उज्ज्वलसारसङ्ग्रहः १

Ujjvala-sāra-saṅgrahaḥ 1

Poems from
Rūpa Gosvāmin's
Blazing Sapphire

Kṛṣṇa Fluting

उज्ज्वलसारसङ्ग्रहः १

Ujjvala-sāra-saṅgrahaḥ 1

Poems from
Rūpa Gosvāmin's
Blazing Sapphire

Vol. 1 (Chapters 1-7)

Selected, edited, translated, introduced, and annotated
by
Neal Delmonico
and
Elizabeth Delmonico

Blazing Sapphire Press
715 E. McPherson
Kirksville, Missouri 63501
2026

Cover design by Russell Nelson

ISBN 978-1-936135-35-6 (1-936135-35-3)

Library of Congress Control Number: 2018938000

Published by:
Blazing Sapphire Press
715 E. McPherson
Kirksville, Missouri 63501

Available at:
Nitai's Bookstore
715 E. McPherson
Kirksville, Missouri, 63501
Phone: (660) 665-0273
http://www.nitaisbookstore.com
http://www.naciketas-press.com
Email: neal@blazing-sapphire-press.com

Images Included in the Book

Cover Image: Rādhā Pining for Kṛṣṇa. From an 18th century Pahari manuscript of the *Gīta-govinda*. From the Freer Gallery of Art and Arthur M. Sackler Gallery, Smithsonian Institution, Washington, D.C.: Gift of Mr. Paul F. Walter, F2005.7

Frontespiece: Kṛṣṇa Fluting. [Companion Persuading Rādhā as Kṛṣṇa Flutes.] From the "Lambagraon" *Gīta-govinda*. India, Himachal Pradesh, Kangra, circa 1825. Los Angeles County Museum of Art. Gift of the Michael J. Connell Foundation (M.71.49.7) The right side of this image is used here, the left side in Chapter 7.

Chapter 1: Kṛṣṇa's Dance of Delight (*Rāsa-līlā*). India, Rajasthan, Bundi, circa 1675-1700. Los Angeles County Museum of Art. Museum Acquisition (M.75.66)

Chapter 2: Kṛṣṇa and His Friends. [Kṛṣṇa and the Cowherds on a Picnic.] Folio from a *Bhāgavata Purāṇa*. India, Himachal Pradesh, Basohli, 1760-1765. Los Angeles County Museum of Art. Gift of the Joseph B. and Ann S. Koepfli Trust in honor of Dr. Pratapaditya Pal (M.2011.156.5)

Chapter 3: Beloved Ladies of Hari. [Kṛṣṇa and Rādhā Enjoying a Feast and Fireworks.] India, Rajasthan, Kishangarh, early 19th century. Los Angeles County Museum of Art. Gift of Jane Greenough Green in memory of Edward Pelton Green (AC1999.127.42)

Chapter 4: Rādhā Lamenting with Her Confidante. From the "Garhwal" *Gīta-govinda*. India, Himachal Pradesh, Kangra, circa 1775-1780. Los Angeles County Museum of Art. Gift of Ramesh and Urmil Kapoor (M.84.222.1)

Chapter 5: Leading Ladies with Kṛṣṇa. [Kṛṣṇa and Gopīs]. India, Pahari, 18th century. National Museum of New Delhi.

Chapter 6: Group Leaders. [Kṛṣṇa, Adored by Ladies, Watched by Monkeys in Trees and by Cattle.] From an album of 18th century Indian watercolours. Bodleian Library, Oxford. MS. Douce Or. a.3 fol31r.

Chapter 7: The Messengers. [Companion Persuading Rādhā as Kṛṣṇa Flutes.] From the "Lambagraon" *Gīta-govinda.* India, Himachal Pradesh, Kangra, circa 1825. Los Angeles County Museum of Art. Gift of the Michael J. Connell Foundation (M.71.49.7) See Frontespiece.

Endpiece: Rādhā and Kṛṣṇa in Each Other's Clothes. India, Himachal Pradesh, Kangra, circa 1800-1825. Los Angeles County Museum of Art. Gift of Corinne and Don Whitaker (M.80.232.4)

Abbreviations

[Thoughout this volume and the following volumes certain abbreviations will occur. A list of those follows:]

Bhāg. *Bhāgavata Purāṇa*

Brs. *Bhakti-rasāmṛta-sindhu* (See also ONSR)

J Jīva Gosvāmin's *Locana-rocanī* (*Pleasing to the Eyes*)

Nś Bharata's *Nāṭya-śāstra* (*Treatise on Drama*)

ONSR *Ocean of the Nectar of Sacred Rapture*

Ras. Siṃhabhūpāla's *Rasārṇava-sudhākara*

Un. Rūpa's *Ujjvala-nīlamaṇi* (*The Blazing Sapphire*)

V Viśvanātha Cakravartin's *Ānanda-candrikā* (*Moonbeam of Bliss*)

VG Viṣṇudāsa Gosvāmin *Svātma-pramodinī* (*Pleasing to My Self*)

Contents

Acknowledgments v

Introduction to the Blazing Sapphire ix

The Author and his Family ix

Rasa and Bhakti-rasa xv

Summary of the Blazing Sapphire xxvi

Kṛṣṇa's Extra-marital Loves? xxxiv

Plagiarism? Rūpa's Use of Siṃhabhūpāla xli

This Collection of Poems xlii

Conclusion xliv

I Text and Translation 1

Chapter One: Varieties of the Hero 3

Chapter Two: Companions of the Hero 33

Chapter Three: The Beloved Ladies of Hari 49

Chapter Four: Śrī Rādhā 67

Chapter Five: Leading Ladies 107

Chapter Six: Faction Leaders 169

Chapter Seven: The Messengers 189

Acknowledgments

Work began on this project many years ago, over thirty years ago, in fact. Thus there are many extraordinary scholars and friends to whom I owe a large debt of gratitude. Many of those who helped me along the way are no longer with us, which makes calling them to memory a specially important responsibility and also a profound pleasure as the first results of this work finally become available. Let me recognize those with whom I studied Sanskrit over the years: Joel A. Erickson (U. of Colorado, 1970), J. Prabhakar Sastri (Andhra University, India, 1978-9), Edwin Gerow (University of Chicago, 1982-3), and Allen Thrasher (University of Chicago, 1987-8). In India I had the good fortune of reading some of the major texts of the Caitanya, Vedanta, and aesthetic traditions with superb Sanskrit scholars like Bisnupada Bhattacarya, Govinda Gopal Mukherjee, Chinmayi Chatterjee, and Minoti Kar. They all in their own brilliant ways provided me with the tools and insights I needed to tackle a complex, sophisticated, multilayered text like the *Ujjvala-nīlamaṇi.*

My interest in the religion and tradition of Śrī Caitanya was created by contact with the movement/society (ISKCON) founded in the USA by A. C. Bhaktivedanta Swami (my involvement was from 1970 to 1976). For a few years I had the good fortune of traveling with him as his Sanskrit secretary in charge of gathering together his early morning dictations, having them typed, editing and confirming them with him, and sending them back to the society's press for publication. Though we disagreed on the role of scholarship in the society and parted on a sour note, I value the time I spent in his society and with him and recognize that he instilled in me an abiding interest in the Caitanya tradition. After I left the society, I joined the disciples of Baba Tinkudi Goswami, whom I regarded as a more traditional and enlightened representative of the larger community of followers of Śrī Caitanya. His kindness and the kindness of his followers nourished and protected me as I lived with them under the sometimes extremely difficult and ascetic conditions that renunciant members of the Caitanya tradition often embrace.

Among those who encouraged me to continue on this project even when my energies and enthusiasm were flagging were Edward C. Dimock while I was a graduate student at the University of Chicago and Srivatsa Goswami of the Sri Radharaman Temple in Vrindaban, India. Goswamiji provided me with copies of many of the major texts of the tradition in the superbly produced editions of Puridas Mahasaya. For access to those texts I am deeply indebted to him.

I am also deeply indebted to Jan K. Brzezinski, aka. Jagat or Jagadananda Das. Long ago he and I started a project on the internet called the Gauḍīya Grantha Mandir (GGM, Temple of the Books of the Caitanya tradition). We wanted to make available all the major works of the Caitanya tradition in the original languages free for all who had an interest in them. It was really Jan who accomplished it, however. He spent days, weeks, months, years, typing in and correcting texts for the archive. I occasionally added a text here and there, but nothing even close to the number and quality of texts Jan contributed. The Sanskrit text included in this volume is based on the one Jan contributed to the GGM. Not only did he type in the main text of the *Ujjvala-nilamaṇi*, he typed in the three available commentaries on the text. For that I am enormously thankful.

Many of my friends and well-wishers have encouraged me over the years and waited patiently while year after year I promised that the translation, which is almost done, would be out soon. Among those are Joseph Knapp, Lloyd Pflueger, Radhapada Das, Sakhicaran Das (now deceased), Malati Dasi, Mark Tinghino, Edwin Bryant, Robert Evans, Lalita Dasi, Haricarana Das, Steven Rosen, Dragoslav Krsmanovic, Radha Sarana Das, Vrnda Devi, and many others.

Next, I must recognize my deep indebtedness to my wife, Elizabeth, and my daughter, Jahnavi Rose. Without Betsy's urging and help over the years I would not have been able finish the current volume. She has believed in it and in me for longer than anyone should have to. In addition, she has taken my clumsy, clunky English renderings of most of the stanzas in this volume and made them shine with a new beauty. Her fine ear for English rhyme and rhythm has emulated to some degree the beauty of Rūpa's original Sanskrit stanzas. She is also responsible for selecting the cream of the crop for this volume. Out of the 400 stanzas in the first seven chapters, she has picked around a hundred that she thought the finest examples of Rūpa's poetic skill for this volume. It is for this reason that I thought she should be listed as translator of this work along side of me.

As for my daughter Jahnavi, she came along a little after my work on this translation started. As I worked on this text, I watched her crawl, walk, run, play, grow, learn, laugh, cry, and transform into the wonderful young lady she has become today, thoughtful and full of kindness. She and this work grew up along side of each other and it was the pleasure I experienced watching her grow up that made working on this translation even more pleasant than it otherwise would have been. They were both labors of love, which is to say they weren't labors at all. This text is not complete; neither is Jahnavi's life. May they both continue to grow and find fulfillment.

Introduction to the Blazing Sapphire

The Author and his Family

The Blazing Sapphire or *Ujjvala-nīlamaṇi* is the work of Rūpa Gosvāmin, a 16th century poet/theologian who was a direct disciple of the Vaiṣṇava reformer Śrī Kṛṣṇa Caitanya of Bengal (1486-1534 CE). We know a few things about Rūpa: he, his elder brother Sanātana, and his younger brother Vallabha, for instance, were ministers in the court of the Nawab (King) Husein Shah, ruler of Bengal (from 1494–1519 CE); Rūpa's was a family of learned brahmins that, according to his nephew Jīva, were once kings in the distant land of Karnataka in South India.[1] They were almost certainly Vaiṣṇava worshippers of Kṛṣṇa before they met Caitanya. As ministers of the Nawab, a Muslim, Rūpa, Sanātana, and Vallabha had probably lost their caste standing and were looking for some way to escape their court duties and devote themselves to the full time pursuit of worship of Kṛṣṇa. Śrī Caitanya provided them with that avenue.

Rūpa and Sanātana met with Caitanya secretly in 1515 CE at a place in Bengal called Rāmakeli—not far from the Nawab's capital—as Cai-

[1]Śrī Jīva gives a history of the family's ancestry at the end of his *Abridged Pleaser of Vaiṣṇavas* (*Laghu-vaiṣṇava-toṣaṇī*), a shortened version of his uncle Sanātana's commentary on the *Bhāgavata Purāṇa*. The passage is also given fully in *The Six Gosvāmīs of Vṛndāvana* (*Vṛndāvanera Chaẏa Gosvāmī*) by Nareśacandra Jānā, pp. 11-13, and Jānā's discussion of the passage is found on pages 13-19. (Calcutta, India: Kalikātā Viśvavidyālaya, 1970)

tanya passed through on his first attempt to make a pilgrimage to the holy land of Vṛndāvana (near Mathurā, in the modern state of Uttar Pradesh), believed to be the place of Kṛṣṇa's childhood.[2] Caitanya asked them to go to Vṛndāvana, write books on the passionate cultivation of love for Kṛṣṇa (*rāgānuga-bhakti*), and uncover the sites where Kṛṣṇa's divine play (*līlā*) is believed to have taken place. Shortly thereafter the three brothers made their escape from the court of the Nawab

Rūpa's Family Tree

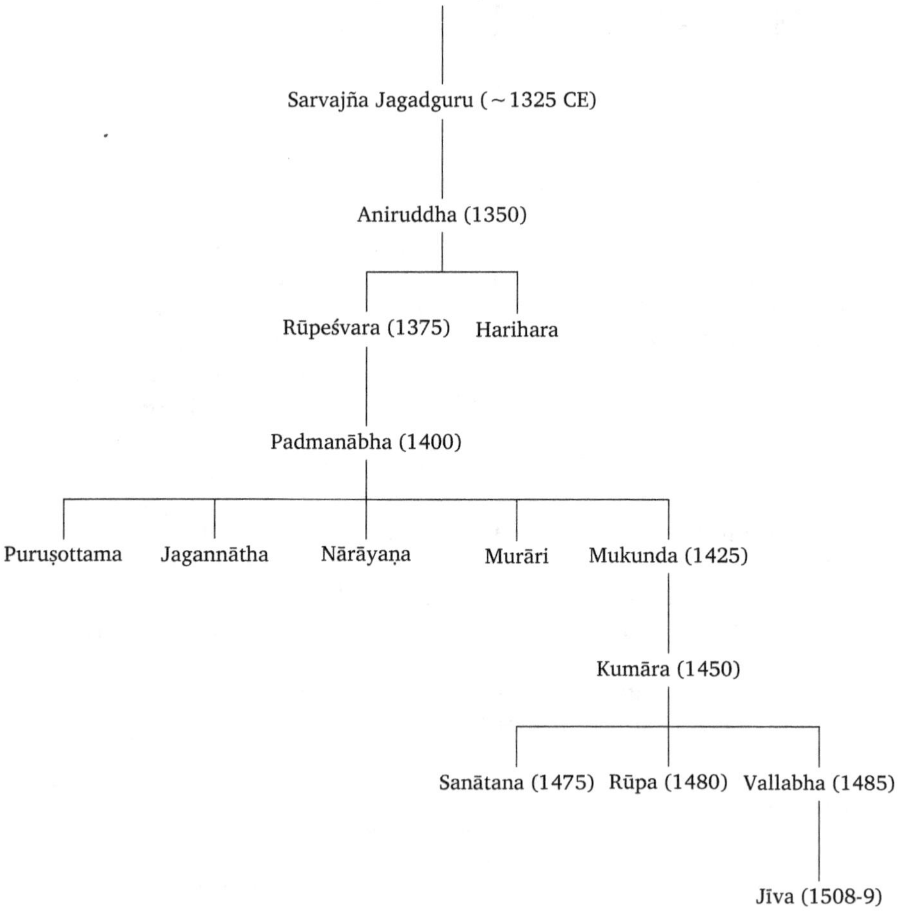

[2]See Nareśacandra Jānā, *Vṛndāvaner Chaya Gosvāmī*, 46, for the date of this meeting.

and made separate runs for Vṛndāvana. Rūpa left first with Vallabha, successfully evading the Nawab's men, and arrived at his destination without being troubled by the Nawab. Sanātana was less fortunate. Since he remained behind, the Nawab, suspecting that he, too, would leave soon, arrested him and threw him in prison for some time. Eventually, he succeeded in convincing a guard to take a substantial bribe and let him go. Once free, he traveled incognito (dressed as an itinerant Sufi, it it said) to Vṛndāvana, connecting again on the way with Caitanya at Vārānasī. The brothers, after short visits to Purī to spend time with Caitanya, lived in Vṛndāvana for the rest of their long lives.[3] The younger brother, Vallabha (aka. Anupama) was probably born in 1485-6. Vallabha's son, Jīva, who joined his uncles in Vṛndāvana sometime before 1541, was probably born in 1508-9 CE. Rūpa, Sanātana, and their nephew Jīva, produced many of the poems, plays, and theological works in Sanskrit that provided the tradition inspired by Caitanya a firm literary and textual foundation.

The Blazing Sapphire is perhaps Rūpa's final work, composed after a lifetime of poetic and dramatic study and practice. It contains fourteen hundred and fifty-one Sanskrit stanzas (*śloka*), some of which are didactic in nature, but most of which are single-stanza poems designed to exemplify and evoke the various complex moods and feelings (*bhakti-rasa*) associated with the tradition's culture of love (*preman*) centered on Kṛṣṇa. Kṛṣṇa is India's god of love before whose beauty and charm all the beauty and love of the world are said to pale. The text, therefore, is not only meant to analyze and to teach about the primary religious experience of the Caitanya tradition, sacred erotic rapture (*madhura-rasa*). It is also meant to provide a poetic vehicle through which it can be experienced by members of the tradition as well. The "sapphire" in the work's name points to the blue-complected Kṛṣṇa, the blue jewel or the sapphire (*nīlamaṇi*); and the quality of "blazing" or "shining brightly" (*ujjvala*) refers to Kṛṣṇa at his brightest and in a state of aroused passion, enflamed with love. Before the *Blazing Sapphire* Rūpa also wrote a number of plays and poems meant to evoke the sacred

[3]The exact dates of the births and deaths of Sanātana and Rūpa are not known. Since Caitanya treated Sanātana as a senior scholar and teacher (See *Caitanya-caritāmṛta*. 3.4.154-155, 161-169) I believe that he was somewhat older than Caitanya, perhaps as many as ten years older, and thus was born around 1475-6 CE. He is thought to have passed away in Vṛndāvana in around 1554-5 CE. Rūpa was younger than Sanātana but slightly older than Caitanya. He was probably born around 1480-1 CE and passed away a couple years after Sanātana in about 1556-7 CE.

rapture experience (*bhakti-rasa*).[4]

In Rūpa's works, divine love (*prema*) is expressed in the language of human love which in turn may be viewed as a pale semblance of the ultimate loving intimacy found in relationship with the divine lord Kṛṣṇa. Thus, from the perspective of this tradition, what we humans seek most thirstily in the many temporal and temporary intimacies of love among other human beings and animals can only be found fully in the intimacy of loving Kṛṣṇa in some relationship. Nothing else really satisfies us. This emotional connection or relationship with Kṛṣṇa is called *bhakti*,[5] and to rejoice in that connection is called sacred rapture or *bhakti-rasa*. That divine relationship contains the prototypical roots of the rich variety of feelings involved in any loving relationship.

This view creates an interesting orientation toward the world in this tradition. The world receives a more positive evaluation by be-

[4]Rūpa's major literary works are the poem *Goose Messenger* (*Haṃsa-dūta*, possibly written before meeting Caitanya in 1515 CE), the poem *Tidings of Uddhava* (*Uddhava-sandeśa*, also possibly written before meeting Caitanya in 1515 CE, but after the *Goose Messenger*), the play *Clever Mādhava* (*Vidagdha-mādhava*, 1532-3 CE), the play *Playful Mādhava* (*Lalita-mādhava*, 1537 CE), and the play *Moonlight on the Sport of Taxing [Rādhā and the Village Milkmaids]* (*Dāna-keli-kaumudī*, 1549 CE). Rūpa also wrote a work on dramaturgy called *Moonlight on Drama* (*Nāṭaka-candrikā*, between 1537-41 CE). In addition to these works Rūpa wrote a number of shorter praises and poetic works that were later collected together by his nephew Jīva into a work called *Garland of Praises* (*Stava-mālā*, probably after Rūpa's death in 1555-6 CE). Rūpa himself anthologized the scattered stanzas of a hundred and twenty-five poets, including a few by himself, his older brother Sanātana, and Caitanya, on various aspects of *bhakti* for Kṛṣṇa in a collection called *Garland of Stanzas* (*Padyāvalī*, sometime before 1541 CE). His other major work on sacred rapture in general was the *Ocean of the Nectar of Sacred Rapture* (*Bhakti-rasāmṛta-sindhu*, completed in 1541 CE).

[5]*Bhakti* is a difficult word to translate into English. It is from the Sanskrit root $\sqrt{bhaj}$ which means "to resort to; to pursue, practise, cultivate; to serve, honour, revere, love, adore." It is often translated into English as devotion, but I find this falls short, because *bhakti* in Sanskrit means much more than that. One is better off surveying the various and sundry ways in which *bhakti* has been defined and understood in the native literature by native scholars. For a small survey of that see the section entitled "Bhakti in Middle" in my introduction to C.C. Caleb's translation of the *Bhagavad-gītā* (*The Divine Song, or Bhagavad-gītā*), xxii-xxvii. (Kirksville, MO: Blazing Sapphire Press, 2012) In brief, however, as Baladeva Vidyābhūṣaṇa (*Jewel of Conclusion, or Siddhānta-ratna*, para. 32) puts it: "*bhakti* is a special kind of knowledge (*bhaktir api jñāna-viśeṣo bhavati*)." To this should be added the actions, feelings, and outlook a person who has this knowledge is led to. We will see this more clearly later in this introduction. Moreover, as Jīva defines it (*Treatise on the Highest Self, Paramātma-sandarbha*, para 92), it is the very core of a special kind of power, a power capable of giving pleasure (the *hlādinī-śakti*) which is capable of subduing even the gods.

ing rooted in divine experience. And yet its inability to satisfy is also accounted for: the principals in all our mundane loving relationships partake of the transitory nature of the things of this world, making relationships between persons and things also transitory. Rūpa's affirmation of the world is a refreshing and unusual orientation in Hinduism, which otherwise has endorsed a strong current of negation and renunciation of the world. As the luscious sensuality present in so many of Rūpa's poems indicates, the relationship with Kṛṣṇa is indeed a sensual and passionate one, but also one thought to be based on eternal bodies (*siddha-dehas*) and eternal identities (*nitya-svarūpas*), not temporary physical bodies or identities. As is illustrated by another work of the tradition, the *Undying Sports of Govinda* (*Govinda-līlāmṛta*) by Kṛṣṇadāsa Kavirāja (1520?-1612?), in Kṛṣṇa's heavenly paradise his play (*līlā*) is eternal. According to this tradition, we, as eternal, conscious beings, each have a place in that eternal play.

Of the various ways of loving Kṛṣṇa recognized by the Caitanya tradition—loving passively as a serene, contemplative sage or *yogī*, loving as a humble servant loves a kind master, loving as a parent loves a clever child, loving as an age-mate friend loves a dear friend, and loving as a lover loves her lover—the highest for Rūpa was this last one called the "sweet one" (*madhura*), loving Kṛṣṇa as a lover, because it affords the greatest degree of intimacy with and surrender to Kṛṣṇa.[6] Although Rūpa has mentioned this way of loving and discussed it briefly in his

---

[6]Rūpa makes this point in his *Ocean of the Nectar of Sacred Rapture* in the following way (2.5.36, 38):

> *mitho harermṛgākṣyāśca sambhogasyādikāraṇam* |
> *madhurāparaparyāyā priyatākhyoditā ratiḥ* |
> *asyāṃ kaṭākṣabhrūkṣepapriyavāṇīsmitādayaḥ* ||*36*||
>
> *yathottaramasau svādaviśeṣollāsamayyapi* |
> *ratirvāsanayā svādvī bhāsate kāpi kasyacit* ||*38*||

"The primary cause of the mutual enjoyment of Hari [Kṛṣṇa] and the doe-eyed ladies of Vraja is the attraction (*rati*) called 'Dearness' (*priyatā*) or 'Sweetness' (*madhura*). In it one finds sidelong glances, eye-brow bending, sweet words, smiles, and so forth."

"That attraction becomes increasingly delightful [tasteful] the later it is [in the order]. One of the forms of this attraction appears tasteful to a person according to that person's memory traces."

Rūpa in this passage of the *Ocean* has listed the forms of attraction to Kṛṣṇa in the following order: as a peaceful contemplative (*śānta*), as a servant (*dāsya*), as a parent or elder (*vātsalya*), as a friend (*sakhya*), and as a lover (*madhura or priyatā*). In the order given, sweet attaction comes last and is thus considered the most flavorful, delicious, or delightful.

earlier work on sacred rapture (*bhakti-rasa*), namely, the *Ocean of the Nectar of Sacred Rapture* (*Bhakti-rasāmṛta-sindhu*), the *Blazing Sapphire* is entirely devoted to elucidating this sweetest way of loving Kṛṣṇa. Rūpa says in the second verse of this text that this way of loving Kṛṣṇa is a secret. And he suggests that the *Blazing Sapphire*, in which this sacred erotic rapture forms the main topic, is a hidden treasure of the followers of Caitanya, among whom Caitanya himself is believed to have revealed and personally embodied this kind of love.[7]

> In this work, erotic rapture (*madhura*), the king of sacred raptures (*bhakti-rasa*), is described separately and in great detail. Because it is secret, it has previously been mentioned only briefly among the main forms of sacred rapture.[8]

Rūpa gives four reasons for avoiding a detailed discussion of this "sweet" way of loving Kṛṣṇa in his earlier work: there is a strong possibility of its being misunderstood; it is secret; it is unsuited for people who are renunciants; and it is a vast topic.[9] This is more evidence that Caitanya Vaiṣṇavism had departed from the long Hindu-Buddhist tradition of prizing renunciation and rejection of the world above all else. The greatest treasure of the Caitanya tradition is not for renunciants, not for *sannyāsins*, those who have renounced family life and worldly affairs in what is typically considered the fourth or last stage of life in the Hindu social order.

---

[7]Rūpa suggests as much in one of the opening stanzas of his play *Clever Mādhava* (*Vidagdha-mādhava*):

> *anarpitacarīṃ cirāt karuṇayāvatīrṇaḥ kalau*
> *samarpayitum unnatojjvalarasāṃ svabhaktiśriyam* |
> *hariḥ puraṭasundaradyutikadambasaṃdīpitaḥ*
> *sadā hṛdayakandare sphuratu vaḥ śacīnandanaḥ* ||

"May the son of Śacī (Caitanya), [who is also] Hari (Kṛṣṇa) and who is radiant with the beautiful glow of gold, forever appear in your hearts. He compassionately has descended in the Age of Kali in order to bestow the treasure of his own *bhakti*—the sublime blazing rapture (sacred erotic rapture)—which had not been given before."

[8]Un., 1.2:

> *mukhya-raseṣu purā yaḥ saṃkṣepeṇodito rahasyatvāt* |
> *pṛthag eva bhakti-rasa-rāṭ sa vistareṇocyate madhuraḥ* ||

[9]Rūpa, *Ocean of the Nectar of Sacred Rasa (ONSR)*, 3.5.2:

> *nivṛttānupayogitvād durūhatvād ayaṃ rasaḥ* |
> *rahasyatvāc ca saṃkṣipya vitatāṅgo'pi likhyate* ||

Rasa and Bhakti-rasa

In structuring his discussion of sacred rapture (*bhakti-rasa*) in general and of sacred erotic rapture (*madhura-rasa*) in particular, Rūpa plugged into the long tradition of reflection on the nature of the experience of drama and poetry in India, a tradition that culminated in the theory of *rasa*, aesthetic pleasure or rapture.[10]

The literary critics of Sanskrit literature have carefully analyzed the process whereby aesthetic rapture (*rasa*) is experienced through literature and art.[11] One should not think of *rasa* as an object of experi-

[10]I use the word rapture because in Viśvanātha Kavirāja's description of *rasa* in his *Mirror of Literature* (*Sāhitya-darpaṇa*), the standard text on *rasa* in the middle ages (14th-15th cents. CE), he describes it as a moment of joyful astonishment that drives all other thoughts and feelings out of the mind. Here is *Sāhitya-darpaṇa*, 3.2:

sattvodrekād akhaṇḍa-svaprakāśānanda-cinmayaḥ
vedyāntara-sparśa-śūnyo brahmāsvāda-sahodaraḥ |
lokottara-camatkāra-prāṇaḥ kaiścit pramātṛbhiḥ
svākāravadabhinnatvenāyam āsvādyate rasaḥ ||

"Out of an upsurge of pure being (*sattva*) it is undivided, self-revealed, joyful consciousness, free from the slighest touch of other objects of awareness, akin to the experience of Brahman, the very life-breath of transcendent astonishment. This rapture (*rasa*) is experienced by some knowers [connoisseurs] as non-different from themselves, like their own bodies."

This understanding of *rasa* is comparable in many ways with Nietzsche's notion of *rausch*. *Rausch* is a German word etymologically related to "rush," but is most commonly translated "frenzy." As "rush" one can imagine the aesthetic state as rushing over one and sweeping one away, dominating one's attention and emotions. So, according to David Farell Krell in a footnote (92, fn) to his translation of Martin Heidegger's work on Nietzsche's conception of art, "rapture" the past participle of *rapere*, "to seize" is a better alternative than "frenzy" for an English translation of *rausch*. One is seized by or taken over by the aesthetic experience. See Heidegger's fascinating study of Nietzsche's aesthetics in *Nietzsche (Volume One): the Will to Power as Art*, especially Chapter 14: Rapture as Aesthetic State. (San Francisco: Harper & Row, 1979)

[11]The earliest expression of the *rasa* theory is found in Bharata's *Treatise on Drama* (*Nāṭya-śāstra*, 4th-5th cent. CE). In the middle of the Sixth Chapter of the text, after verse 31, one finds two aphorisms on *rasa* which suggests, since they stand out from the rest of the text by not being in meter, that they are carried over from an earlier text or author. The first is the famous aphorism on rapture (*rasa-sūtra*) which establishes the centrality of rapture (*rasa*) in the aesthetic experience and indeed in the Sanskrit tradition of literary criticism: *na hi rasād ṛte kaścid arthaḥ pravartate*, "Without *rasa* no meaning or purpose arises [in the literary arts]." The second aphorism describes how *rasa* is thought to arise: *tatra vibhāvānubhāva-vyabhicāri-saṃyogād rasa-niṣpattiḥ*, "From the conbination of stimulants, consequents, and transitory emotions, *rasa* is created." Another component discussed in Bharata, the enduring emotion (*sthāyibhāva*), is surprisingly absent from Rūpa's formulation. It is brought to mind by the proper coordination of the stimulants,

ence, however. *Rasa is* the experience itself. Sanskrit literary critics have analyzed the elements of aesthetic experience into the following categories: stimulants (*vibhāvas*) or causes; consequents (*anubhāvas*) or effects; autonomous physical effects (*sāttvika-bhāvas*); and transitory emotions (*vyabhicāri-bhāvas*) or fleeting emotions. When these are skillfully represented in works of art, particular associated emotions are evoked from residual memory traces[12] of audience members and become powerfully present to them once again. Those emotions, however, are now shorn of their original occasions or contexts. Freed from those real life situations of the past, they are experienced anew, detached from any particular time, place, or identity, and are renamed *rasa* to distinguish them from ordinary, everyday emotional experiences, which are called *bhāvas*, or "feeling-states." The freeing of the emotions from their original contexts and occasions is called generalization (*sādhāraṇībhāvanā*). Skillful portrayal of emotional situations in literature causes them to be awakened and generalized and they thus become enjoyable. Such is the mainstream version of the *rasa* theory as expounded by Abhinavagupta (11th cent. CE) of Kaśmīra.[13]

In addition, among early writers on aesthetic rapture (*rasa*) a strong link was recognized between aesthetic experience and religious experience, especially in the case of the non-dual experience called *brahmāsvāda*, tasting Brahman, the impersonal absolute. Abhinavagupta, discussing the theories of his predecessors in his build-up to his own more fully formulated theory, refers to this impersonal-absolute ex-

---

consequents, and transitory emotions. On the transitory emotions that go with the erotic *rasa*, see *The Nāṭya Śāstra of Bharatamuni*, trans. into English by a Board of Scholars, 76. (Delhi, India: Sri Satguru Publications, 1987).

[12]By residual memory traces I mean the *vāsanās* or *saṃskāras*. In Hindu psychology these refer to traces or impressions left in the fabric of the mind by powerful emotional experiences from one's past. These are the basis of memories, of inclinations for or against various things. These are what in the West would be called "instincts," but in India they are considered survivals from past-life experiences, either in this birth or in previous births. The emotional traces preserved in a person's mind are awakened by the specific stimulants and consequents portrayed in literature that are connected with the emotions that created those traces. When awakened they are shorn of their original occasions and are re-experienced during the presentation of the play, free of any of the unpleasant side-effects those experiences may have occasioned when they were experienced in ordinary life.

[13]Abhinavagupta presents his understanding of *rasa* in his commentaries on verse 1.18 of *Light on Suggestion* (*Dhvany-āloka*) of Ānandavardhana (9th cent. CE) and on the aphorism on *rasa* which appears in an unnumbered prose section (between 6.31 and 6.32) in Bharata's (4th cent. CE) *Treatise on Drama* (*Nāṭya-śāstra*).

perience which had been articulated by a predecessor named Bhaṭṭa Nāyaka in the 9th (?) century.[14] Bhaṭṭa Nāyaka taught, according to Abhinavagupta, that *rasa*, when it is revealed by a special function of language (*bhāvakatva*), which is different from denotation, becomes enjoyed in a special kind of way different from direct experience, memory, and so forth. This *rasa*, due to an emergent state of goodness (*sattva*), is pervaded by joy and light, and is deeply enjoyed with an enjoyment closely akin to the experience (*āsvāda*, tasting) of Supreme Brahman.[15]

It is not too surprising, then, to see Rūpa turn to aesthetic theory to try to describe and validate the religious experience of his tradition. Abhinavagupta and Rūpa, however, both differ from Bhaṭṭa Nāyaka in their thinking about the relationship between aesthetic and religious experiences. For them the experiences are similar, but not the same. According to Rūpa, the religious experience is not a temporary experience, but one that is permanently transformative and that continues to deepen and intensify over time. It is so because it occurs on a foundation the experiencer believes to be her true and eternal identity, his true and eternal nature, not on the basis of impermanent, unreal conceptions of self based on the physical body. The mechanism for evoking or inducing both experiences, however, is quite similar. The primary emotion, known by the technical term stable or enduring emotion (*sthāyibhāva*),[16] is presented in plays and poems through descriptions of its

[14]This is found in his commentary on the aphorism about *rasa* (*rasa-sūtra*) in Bharata's *Treatise on Drama* (*Nāṭya-śāstra*, 6.32).

[15]*Abhinava-bhāratī*, [Gnoli, 10; Nś, 273]: *vibhāvādi-sādhāraṇīkaraṇātmanābhidāto dvitīyenāṃśena bhāvakatva-vyāpāreṇa bhāvyamāno raso'nubhava-smṛty-ādi-vilakṣaṇena … sattvodreka-prakāśānanda-maya-nija-saṃvid-viśrānti-lakṣaṇena parabrahmāsvāda-savidhena bhogena paraṃ bhujyata iti*

[16]In classical Sanskrit literary criticism there are eight or nine enduring emotions, that is, emotions that are powerful enough and central enough in real human experience to power an entire play or poem, or at least a sizable portion of one. These are: love, mirth, sorrow, anger, energy (vitality), terror, disgust, and astonishment. The ninth stable emotion, dispassion or indifference (*nirveda*), was added later. These emotions are represented in art and are enjoyed. To indicate their different effects on human beings when represented in art, they are given different names. These are: the erotic, comic, pathetic, furious, heroic, terrifying, odious, and wonderful. The ninth is the peaceful.

Rūpa's sacred rapture (*bhakti-rasa*) takes as its enduring emotion, delight in Kṛṣṇa or *kṛṣṇa-rati*, which is an adaptation of love or *rati*, the first enduring emotion from classical Sanskrit aesthetics. Rūpa takes it as the primary (*mukhya*) enduring emotion in his sacred aesthetics and, as we have said before, he divides it into five types that ascend in intensity and intimacy. The other seven enduring emotions from classical aesthetics are demoted

proper stimulants or causes (*vibhāva*, a handsome young man and beautiful woman, a moonlit night, fragrant aromas carried on the gentle breezes, distant romantic music, etc. for the erotic *rasa*, for instance), consequents or results of stimulation (*anubhāva*, sidelong glances, lowering one's eyes, looking down at one's feet, smiling, speaking inaudibly, stuttering, etc), and transitory emotions (*vyabhicāri-bhāva*, envy, inebriation, anxiety, bashfulness, joyfulness, etc.). These are expressed either in language, or through gesture, or in any other artistic medium. The primary emotion is thus made tangible or present to the mind and capable of being enjoyed by sensitive members of the audience. If all goes well—in other words, if the viewer or auditor is able to overcome the various obstacles to full engagement[17]—and if the presentation is skillfully crafted and flawlessly executed, the resulting experience is overwhelming and absorbs the full and sustained attention of the viewer, possibly causing in him or her autonomic reactions like tears, trembling, horripilation, fainting, and others.[18]

Abhinavagupta concludes that in the *rasa* experience consciousness

---

to secondary status (*gauṇa*) and figure in as minor players in Rūpa's religious aesthetics, more akin the transitory emotions than enduring emotions. Delight in Kṛṣṇa is not like the other enduring emotions based on memory traces of common human experiences, however. It enters the human psyche as a result of the performance of religious rites and practices related to the worship of and cultivation of love for Kṛṣṇa. Alternatively, one gains it by sheer good luck through the grace of Kṛṣṇa or by crossing paths with one of his dear *bhaktas*. Once it appears in the psyche it operates like the other enduring emotions.

[17]In his discussion of *rasa* (*Abhinava-Bhāratī*, 282-286) Abhinavagupta lists and discusses in detail seven obstacles to the *rasa* experience in literature. These are: (1) lack of verisimilitude in the work, (2) immersion in one's own temporal and spatial determinations during the performance of or engagement with the work, (3) being distracted by one's own sensations of pleasure, etc. during the performance, (4) defective perception of the work, (5) lack of evidence, that is to say, not having perceived the work directly oneself, but instead through someone else's testimony or through inference, (6) absence of a predominant factor, that is, not finding a dominant or enduring emotion in the work, and (7) the presence of doubt about the dominant or enduring emotion of the work. These seven factors prevent the experience of aesthetic rapture.

[18]These are called the *sāttvika-bhāvas*, uncontrollable physical expressions caused by powerful inner feelings. There are eight of these. Rūpa lists these in his *Ocean of the Nectar of Sacred Rapture* (2.3.16). His verse is almost exactly the same as the verse in Bharata's *Treatise on Drama* over a thousand years earlier (6.22):

> *stambhaḥ svedo'tha romāñcaḥ svarabhaṅgo'tha vepathuḥ* |
> *vaivarṇyamaśru pralaya ityaṣṭau sāttvikāḥ smṛtāḥ* ||

"Paralysis, perspiration, goose-bumps, cracking of the voice, trembling, discoloration, tears, and fainting; these are the eight *sāttvikas*."

briefly rises above its delimiters and shines freely and joyfully, colored only by the subtle memeory trace of the enduring emotion evoked by the play or poem. He agrees with his predecessor, Bhaṭṭa Nāyaka, who viewed the aesthetic experience as similar to the experience of Supreme Brahman (*parama-brahmāsvāda*), the absolute, a difference being that the aesthetic experience is temporary and incomplete while the experience of Brahman is considered permanent, transformative, and complete.

In Rūpa's hands aesthetic rapture (*rasa*) is replaced by sacred rapture (*bhakti-rasa*), a religious experience evoked, as with aesthetic pleasure, through poetry, drama, and other arts. One major difference is that sacred rapture is evoked in response to works featuring stories about the gods, specifically in Rūpa's case, stories about Kṛṣṇa and his companions. But this is not the only or even the most important difference. In the third stanza of his *Blazing Sapphire* he gives a general account of the evocation of sacred erotic rapture:

> When the type of love (*rati*) called sweet (*madhura*, i.e. erotic) becomes enjoyable through expression [in literature] of the stimulants, and the rest (*vibhāvas*, etc.), it becomes the kind of sacred rapture (*bhakti-rasa*) the wise call sweet.[19]

This stanza demonstrates that Rūpa understood and for the most part accepted the classical formulation of aesthetic rapture. Emotions when portrayed in literature are experienced differently from those we experience in our daily lives. Emotions portrayed in literature become generalized (*sādhāraṇībhūta*) and touch us in different ways and on deeper levels than emotions experienced in daily life.[20] For Rūpa and those who follow him, when emotions are portrayed as Kṛṣṇa's or as those of his lovers or companions, one not only has an opportunity for aesthetic experience (*rasa*), one also and more importantly for the Caitanya tradition, has a chance for a profound religious experience

---

[19]Rūpa, *Blazing Sapphire*, 1.3:

> *vakṣyamāṇair vibhāvādyaiḥ svādyatāṃ madhurā ratiḥ* |
> *nītā bhatirasaḥ prokto madhurākhyo manīṣibhiḥ* ||

[20]Compare this view with Jeffrey Zacks' recent work on the neuroscience of film. He says drama gives viewers distilled, condensed, refined emotional experiences. *Flicker: Your Brain on Movies.* (Oxford: Oxford University Press, 2014)

(*bhakti-rasa*), provided one is able to connect with the subject matter of the poem or play in a special way. In other words, we can see Kṛṣṇa as just an ordinary hero or leading character (*nāyaka*) in a poem or play, and experience aesthetic rapture on the basis of our own residual memory traces (*vāsanās*) brought to consciousness and generalized by the descriptive and plot elements of the work (i.e., through the stimulants, consequents, physical consequents, and transitory emotions). Or, if one possesses a special kind of memory trace called *bhakti* or delight in Kṛṣṇa (*kṛṣṇa-rati*), one will taste a special kind of pleasure and enchantment not available to those audience members who do not have that trace. In the case of those with the *bhakti*-trace, it is not generalization that transforms an ordinary residual emotional trace into aesthetic rapture. Rather, it is the presence of this special emotional trace that, when raised to consciousness, is experienced as sacred rapture. Art then becomes a vehicle for religious experience for those who have that special *bhakti*-trace. Aesthetic experience or rapture arises from generalization of residual traces of ordinary emotions; sacred rature arises from the raising to consciousness of a special, non-ordinary, and rarely present emotional trace.

Rūpa describes rather poetically how this special emotional trace, which he calls simply *bhāva*, descends into the heart of a *bhakta*.[21] In his earlier work, the *Ocean of the Nectar of Sacred Rapture* (1.3.1), he writes:

> A special kind of pure being (*śuddha-sattva*), which, equal to a ray from the sun of divine love (*preman*), softens someone's mind through its splendor, is called the [enduring] emotion (*bhāva*, aka. *sthāyi-bhāva*) [of sacred rapture].[22]

And then shortly thereafter, Rūpa describes how this "ray" of the "sun" of divine love enters into and becomes part of the psyche of the *bhakta* (1.3.4-5):

> Appearing among the contents of the mind, it becomes one of them. Though it is by nature self-revealing it appears

[21]*Bhakta* is the term for one who either already has this *bhakti*-trace or who is striving through various practices to gain it.

[22]Rūpa, ONSR, 1.3.1:

> *śuddha-sattva-viśeṣātmā prema-sūryāṃśu-sāmya-bhāk |*
> *rucibhiś citta-māsṛṇyakṛd asau bhāva ucyate ||*

> as if it is revealed. Though that delight is actually by its very nature enjoyment itself, it becomes the cause of the enjoyment of Kṛṣṇa and his companions.[23]

This enduring emotion, delight in Kṛṣṇa, is the basis of sacred rapture. According to Rūpa it is born in two ways: by concentrated practice or cultivation of *bhakti*[24] and by the grace of either Kṛṣṇa or one of his *bhaktas* who has it. The first way is the more common way of acquiring this trace. The second way is very rare. Those who obtain it in either way, says Rūpa, are extremely fortunate.[25]

Rūpa discusses again the enduring emotion as a residual trace later in his *Ocean of the Nectar of Sacred Rapture*. There he gives a more complete description of how that new trace in the heart of the *bhakta* becomes enjoyed or, to put it differently, how it becomes sacred rapture (*bhakti-rasa*). At the same time, Rūpa throws a kind of interesting twist into the picture. Here is what he says (2.1.5.):

> By the stimulants, the consequents, the autonomous physical consequents (tears, trembling, goose-bumps, etc., physical forms of the consequents), and the transitory emotions,

---

[23]Rūpa, ONSR, 1.3.4-5:

> *āvirbhūya mano-vṛttau vrajantī tat-svarūpatām* |
> *svayaṃ-prakāśa-rūpāpi bhāsamānā prakāśyavat* ||
> *vastutaḥ svayam-āsvāda-svarūpaiva ratis tv asau* |
> *kṛṣṇādi-karmakāsvāda-hetutvaṃ pratipadyate* ||

[24]Rūpa in his *Ocean of the Nectar of Sacred Rapture* gives a description of sixty-four practices that are conducive to the appearance of this enduring emotion (*bhāva*, or delight in Kṛṣṇa *kṛṣṇa-rati*) (1.2.97-237). At the end of that lengthy account, however, Rūpa says (1.2.238):

> *durūhādbhutavīrye'smin śraddhā dūre'stu pañcake* |
> *yatra svalpo'pi sambandhaḥ saddhiyāṃ bhāvajanmane* ||
> No need is there for faith in these last five;
> there is strength in them, amazing
> and difficult to conceive of, since
> even slight connection with them
> leads to the birth of *bhāva.*

The last five (60-64) of the sixty-four practices of *bhakti* are: taking pleasure in serving the sacred images of Kṛṣṇa, tasting the meanings of the *Bhāgavata Purāṇa*, keeping the company of *bhaktas* of the lord whose dispositions and affections are similar to one's own, singing aloud the holy names of the lord, and residing in the lord's holy land (Mathurā and its surrounding areas collectively known as Vraja, 1.2.225-237).

[25]Rūpa, ONSR, 1.3.6.

> this enduring emotion, delight in Kṛṣṇa, becomes enjoyable in the hearts of *bhaktas* through hearing and so forth [i.e., through literature] and becomes sacred rapture.[26]

Here Rūpa mentions all the elements in poetry or plays that contribute to raising an enduring emotion to its higher status of conscious enjoyment as sacred rapture. But what form does this enduring emotion have in the heart of a *bhakta*? This he tells us in the next five verses (2.1.6-10):

> Those whose true *bhakti* traces come from both their past life [or, lives] and their present lives have the enjoyment of sacred rapture take birth in their hearts.
>
> In those whose faults have been cleansed away by *bhakti*, whose minds are pleased and luminous, who are attached to the *Bhāgavata Purāṇa*, who enjoy the company of *rasikas* (enjoyers of sacred rapture), whose very lives have become real treasures of the pleasure of *bhakti* to the feet of Govinda [Kṛṣṇa], and who perform acts that are essential to divine love—in the hearts of such *bhaktas* shines a delight that is set aflame by two traces (past and present), a delight which, though it is joy itself, is brought to a state of ever deeper enjoyment.
>
> That delight reaches the highest state of astonishment and intense joy when the stimulants, consequents, and transitory emotions, in other words, Kṛṣṇa and the rest, enter into such *bhaktas*' awarenesses. [27]

---

[26]ibid., 2.1.5:

> *vibhāvair anubhāvaiś ca sāttvikair vyabhicāribhiḥ |*
> *svādyatvaṃ hṛdi bhaktānām ānītā śravaṇādibhiḥ |*
> *eṣā kṛṣṇa-ratiḥ sthāyī bhāvo bhakti-raso bhavet ||*

[27]Rūpa, ONSR, 2.1.6-10:

> *prāktany ādhunikī cāsti yasya sad-bhakti-vāsanā |*
> *eṣa bhakti-rasāsvādas tasyaiva hṛdi jāyate ||*
> *bhakti-nirdhuta-doṣāṇām prasannojjvala-cestasām |*
> *śrībhāgavata-raktānāṃ rasikāsaṅga-raṅgiṇām ||*
> *jīvanībhūta-govinda-pāda-bhakti-sukha-śriyām |*
> *premāntaraṅga-bhūtāni kṛtayāny evānutiṣṭhatām ||*
> *bhaktānāṃ hṛdi rājantī saṃskārayugalojjvalā |*

From this passage it is clear that two special *bhakti* traces are evoked when viewing or auditing plays or poems about Kṛṣṇa and his playful interactions with his companions. As we saw before, those traces are produced by determined engagement in the various practices connected with the cultivation of *bhakti,* or more rarely, by the grace of Kṛṣṇa or one of his dear *bhaktas* who has them. Apparently, having a trace created by one's present *bhakti* practices is not enough to bring about the experience of sacred rapture. The trace created by present practice needs to be augmented and strengthened by a trace created by practices from a previous life or lives. Then, the combined traces together are experienced as sacred rapture.

All of Rūpa's remarks so far apply to the enduring emotion, delight in Kṛṣṇa, *kṛṣṇa-rati,* In the next stanza Rūpa refers to divine love, *preman.* He distinguishes the enduring emotion from divine love in this way (2.1.11):

> But, divine love, being led to even the smallest state of determination by even the slightest presence of stimulants and the rest, may suddenly become tasted as sacred rapture.[28]

Divine love is much stronger than the enduring emotion. The enduring emotion is considered just the bud of divine love. It requires two traces plus fully developed and skillfully expressed stimulants, consequents, autonomous physical consequents, and transitory emotions to be enjoyed as sacred rapture. Divine love, however, becomes enjoyed as sacred rapture at even the slightest hint of stimulants and so forth. Rūpa had suggested this difference when he applied the metaphor of the sun and its rays to the two as he introduced the rise of the enduring emotion quoted above. Divine love is like the sun and the enduring emotion is like just a ray of that sun. A ray of the sun of divine love softens the mind or heart, but the divine love as the sun melts it completely. Rūpa says (1.4.1):

> *ratir ānandarūpaiva nīyamānā tu rasyatām ||*
> *kṛṣṇādibhir vibhāvādyair gatair anubhavādhvani |*
> *prauḍānanda-camatkārakāṣṭhām āpadyate parām ||*

[28]Rūpa, ONSR, 2.1.11:

> *kintu premā vibhāvādyaiḥ svalpair nīto'py anīyasīm |*
> *vibhāvanāvasthāṃ tu sadya āsvādyatāṃ vrajet ||*

> Condensed enduring emotion that completely melts the heart
> and that is marked by extreme possessiveness [toward Kṛṣṇa]
> the wise call divine love.[29]

Divine love (*preman*) is a condensed, more powerful form of the enduring emotion, delight in Kṛṣṇa (*kṛṣṇa-rati*). It grows out of the enduring emotion as the latter grows and strengthens over time and eventually reaches a point at which a sense of possessiveness toward Kṛṣṇa (He is mine!) is felt. This *preman* overpowers a person's sense of possessiveness toward other people and things. This strengthened and more sensitive form of the enduring emotion as divine love has ramifications for the experience of sacred rapture. Since it rises to sacred rapture at the slightest presence of stimulants, it is no longer dependent on well-conceived and skillfully executed literature to give it a lift. The presence of divine love in a *bhakta's* heart can bring about sacred rapture by merely hearing a flute played while walking somewhere, or seeing the blue-gray color of a rain cloud in the distance, or seeing a peacock feather fluttering in the wind. All of these and many other things besides are stimulants which when appearing in a play or poem would evoke sacred rapture. Here, however, they appear as part of a person's experience in the world. The whole world then becomes filled with potential stimulants, consequents, and transitory emotions that are capable of boosting one who has divine love into states of sacred rapture at any moment. What is more, beyond divine love there are several more developed and intense forms of the enduring emotion that are defined and discussed in the fourteenth chapter of the *Blazing Sapphire*.[30] Those will be fully discussed and exemplified in volume

---

[29]Rūpa, ONSR, 1.4.1:

> *samyaṅmasṛṇita-svānto mamatvātiśayāṅkitaḥ* |
> *bhāvaḥ sa eva sāndrātmā budhaiḥ premā nigadyate* ||

[30]Beyond *preman* are even higher, more powerful conditions of the enduring emotion: *sneha* (tenderness), *māna* (an affected sulking), *praṇaya* (confidence), *rāga* (passion that turns sorrow into joy), *anurāga* (ever fresh love), *bhāva* (selfless love such as only the village ladies, the *gopīs*, have for Kṛṣṇa). This is also called the "great" love or *mahābhāva* to distinguish it from the ordinary emotions of most everyday lives. Most of these higher conditions (*vilāsas*) Rūpa has borrowed from Siṃhabhūpāla's (14th cent. CE) *Moon of the Ocean of Aesthetic Rapture* (*Rasārṇava-sudhākara*, 2.111-123ab). Siṃhabhūpāla in turn got them, or some of them, from Bhojarāja's (11th cent. CE) *Light on Erotic Love* (*Śṛṅgāra-prakāśa*) or perhaps from his earlier *Necklace of the Goddess of Poetry* (*Sarasvatī-kaṇṭhābharaṇa*). Rūpa's close following of Siṃhabhūpāla's work and his relationship

three of this work.

This, then, is the way Rūpa adapted the mainstream literary critical theory of how aesthetic pleasure arises in the experience of literature to illuminate the primary religious experience of his own budding tradition. Instead of evoking ordinary memory traces of powerful past emotional experiences as aesthetic rapture does, sacred rapture is based on special non-ordinary memory traces that are built up through participation in religious rites and practices connected with Kṛṣṇa worship in this life and in previous lives. The purpose of those rites and practices is calling to mind Kṛṣṇa and his companions. As Kṛṣṇa is called to mind repeatedly over time, impressions of him, his character, his companions, his names, and his acts begin to build up and memory traces are formed, gradually getting stronger over time. Eventually, the enduring emotion appears in the mind of the practitioner, appearing like a ray of light from the radiant sun of divine love. That ray—delight in Kṛṣṇa (*Kṛṣṇa-rati*) strengthened by the memory traces built up by practice—is raised to awareness by the artful portrayal of suitable stimulants, consequents, autonomic physical consequents, and transitory emotions in works of literature about Kṛṣṇa and his supernatural deeds. The practitioner thus experiences sacred rapture.

Theologically speaking, the ray of light that appears in the mind of the practitioner is an aspect of a divine power that the Caitanya tradition calls the pleasure-giving power of Kṛṣṇa, or the *hlādinī śakti.* Kṛṣṇa experiences pleasure through the pleasure-giving power and bestows pleasure on others through that same power.[31] When it takes its place in the heart of the *bhakta* it gives him or her pleasure whenever Kṛṣṇa or people and things related to him become objects of experience. Similarly, when the *bhakta* is an object of Kṛṣṇa's experience Kṛṣṇa receives pleasure.[32] A powerful resource, however, for the experience of Kṛṣṇa and the pleasure it brings to *bhaktas* is literature.

---

with Bhojarāja's work will be discussed in later volumes of the *Ujjvala-sāra-saṅgraha.* The "great emotion" (*mahābhāva*) and its varieties are Rūpa's own additions to these conditions.

[31]Rūpa's nephew Jīva proposes this in his *Treatise on the Lord* (*Bhagavat-sandarbha*), paragraph 117: *hlādaka-rūpo 'pi bhagavān yayā hlādate hlādayati ca sā hlādinī.* "The Lord, though the embodiment of pleasure himself, takes pleasure and gives pleasure through her, the pleasure-giving power."

[32]See Kanupriya Gosvāmī's discussion of this interrelationship based on the pleasure-giving power in his *On Associating with Great Ones*, 35-40. (Kirksville, Missouri: Blazing Sapphire Press, 2014)

Summary of the Blazing Sapphire

Chapter One of the *Blazing Sapphire*, which has forty-three stanzas, is about the hero, the leading man (*nāyaka*), or in the context of love poetry, the lover. In Rūpa's dramatic and poetic world Kṛṣṇa is the only hero. The hero is one of the stimulants (*vibhāva*), specifically a "supporting" stimulant (*ālambana-vibhāva*), the first of the "ingredients" of the *rasa* experience. This chapter describes the various types of hero, drawing from the literature of Sanskrit aesthetics, and introducing Kṛṣṇa in his various roles as the embodiment of each type. The major distinction drawn in this chapter is between Kṛṣṇa as husband (*pati*) and Kṛṣṇa as paramour (*upapati*). His role as husband is only briefly described with the help of a few examples. Rūpa gives the lion's share of his attention and examples to Kṛṣṇa as paramour. Rūpa defends this focus against the reservations of the earlier Sanskrit literary critics who favored the husband, by insisting that Kṛṣṇa is not an ordinary hero. We will have more to say on this topic later in this introduction.

In Chapter Two, which has twenty-three stanzas, Rūpa describes the hero's closest male friends, his confidants, and helpers (*sahāya*) who assist Kṛṣṇa in arranging and bringing his love affairs to fruition. They are divided into five categories: the trusted servant-friend, the parasite, the jester, the accomplice, and the dear playmate. They are also a kind of supporting stimulant in the sweet sacred rapture.

In chapters three through nine Rūpa describes the beautiful women or heroines (lit. *nāyikā* or leading ladies) of the cowherd village who love Kṛṣṇa. They are also counted among the "supporting" stimulants. The supporting stimulants, however, are now subdivided into two groups: the objects of love (*viṣaya*), those who are loved, that is, Kṛṣṇa in his various roles; and the subjects of love (*āśraya*), or those who possess or feel love for him, i.e., the ladies of the cowherder village. In other words, the person (Kṛṣṇa) who is loved is the object of love and the persons who do the loving, the village women, are the subjects of love. It is worth noting here that the male friends of Kṛṣṇa are not consided objective supporting stimulants (*viṣaya-ālambana-vibhāvas*). They merely help Kṛṣṇa by assisting him in matters of dress, in the arts of making love, in acting as messengers to the village ladies on his behalf, or as his dear confidants. According to Jīva, they are eunuchs, devoid of maleness, and thus have no erotic interest themselves in Kṛṣṇa's love affairs.[33] With Chapter Three we move away from a description of the object of love, Kṛṣṇa, to the subjects of love, the ladies of the cowherder village. Each chapter following that is devoted to a different aspect of the natures, qualities, and interactions of the heroines who love Kṛṣṇa.

In Chapter Three, which has sixty-one stanzas, Rūpa describes in general terms the ladies who love Kṛṣṇa. It includes two major types: those who are his wives (in his capital city, Dvārakā, where he lived with his queens, or those village ladies in Vraja who thought of him as their husband)[34] and those who are his extra-marital lovers (primarily the ladies of Vraja who were married to others). Rūpa argues for the superiority of the extra-marital type of love because the hidden or secretive nature of the passion and the difficulty of gaining access to the beloved lady are very pleasing to Kṛṣṇa.[35] Rūpa also warns against ordinary men trying to imitate the supremely powerful Kṛṣṇa.[36]

In Chapter Four, which has fifty-five stanzas, the focus is on Rādhā, who is the most beautiful, most qualified, and most clever of the ladies who love Kṛṣṇa. Her qualities such as her sweetness, her youth, the quickness of her side-long glances and the rest, are given and each is exemplified with a poem. Towards the end of this chapter Rādhā's five types of female friends (like Kṛṣṇa's five types of male friend/helpers in Chapter Two) are described.

Chapter Five, which has one hundred and three stanzas, is where Rūpa describes the lovers of Kṛṣṇa as female heroes or leading ladies (*nāyikās*) drawing from some of the insights of traditional Sanskrit literary criticism. In this chapter the heroines are characterized as of three types: young and innocent (*mugdhā*); a little older and in the middle between innocent and experienced (*madhyā*); and more mature and experienced (*pragalbhā*). Towards the end of the chapter the eight archetypal situations in which heroines find themselves in their relationships with Kṛṣṇa are described and exemplified. These situations include, for example, a heroine on her way to a secret night meeting with Kṛṣṇa in the forest, or one who is finely dressed and waiting ex-

---

[33]Jīva Gosvāmin, *Locana-rocanī,* 2.1

[34]Their prayer to the goddess Kātyāyanī asking her to make Kṛṣṇa their husband is cited at Un., 1.14. It is a verse taken from the *Bhāgavata Purāṇa* (10.22.44). Though no ritual marriages took place some among the girls considered Kṛṣṇa their husband.

[35]Un., 3.19.

[36]Ibid., 3.24-5.

pectantly for Kṛṣṇa to come to her pleasingly decorated bower.

In Chapter Six, which has twenty-six stanzas, Rūpa describes the group-leaders among the heroines. That the ladies of Vraja are organized into innumerable groups of varying sizes, and that each group has a dominant leader, was mentioned at the beginning of Chapter Five. Now, in Chapter Six, these group leaders are described in terms of their good fortune (*saubhāgya*) with respect primarily to their love for Kṛṣṇa, but also in reference to their beauty, sweetness, cleverness, and other good qualities. By the measure of these traits they may be either surpassing (*adhika*), average (*sama*), or minimal (*laghu*). Moreover, heroines may be subdivided into three categories descriptive of their natures: harsh or sharp-tongued (*prakharā*); middling or equable (*madhyā*); and soft or mild-mannered (*mṛdvī*). To these relatively fortunate or unfortunate ladies are added two absolutes: the absolutely most fortunate, and the absolutely least fortunate. Altogether, Rūpa says, there are twelve varieties of group leader.[37]

In Chapter Seven, which has ninety-six stanzas, Rūpa focuses on the trusted female messengers of Vraja—the individuals who discretely carry messages back and forth between the village ladies and Kṛṣṇa. In this chapter, however, Rūpa first names and illustrates another kind of message-sending, namely that which is done by the lady's own movements, glances, gestures, and tone of voice, and by her direct and indirect verbal cues. While these self-sent messages can be deeply moving, most of this chapter's examples involve the roles of other messengers. The role is often played by female artists, astrologers, female ascetics, maidservants, and girlfriends—and by Vṛndā, the goddess of the forest Vṛndāvana. Rūpa provides illustrations of these messengers in action, dividing them into three varieties depending upon how much they are trusted to skillfully do. Some messengers, the *amitārthā*, are unlimited in their roles as conveyors of their friend's wishes; some, the less skilled *nisṛṣṭārthā*, are entrusted with a single task. And some messengers, the *patrahārikā*, are simply letter-carriers.

Chapter Eight, which has a hundred and thirty-seven stanzas, deals

[37]The math may seem odd here and it kind of is. There are two absolutes and nine relatives: the absolute more, the absolute lesser, the three types of relative mores, three types of relative averages, and three types of lessers. That adds up to eleven types of group leaders. However, Rūpa points out that in the case of the absolute lesser, while there are many who have more than she, there are also others who are equal to her. Therefore, there are two types of absolute lesser: the absolute lesser and those who are equal to her.

with the types and roles of the female friends (*sakhīs*) of the group leaders. Leaders and their friends make up groups which compete with each other for the attention and love of Kṛṣṇa. Rūpa categorizes the leaders' friends in much the same way as he had the leaders themselves in Chapter Six. They may be highly fortunate, moderately fortunate, or relatively unfortunate primarily in love for Kṛṣṇa, but also in beauty, sweetness, and wit. They are thus known as surpassing, average, or minimal depending on which of the three categories of fortune they fall into. By nature, they may be overly aggressive, or they may be overly timid, or they may be nicely balanced between those extremes. Examples abound for each of these nine types of friends. And in addition to these nine categories, Rūpa defines and exemplifies two special categories—the "absolutely most fortunate" and "absolutely least fortunate" of women. Friends deliver messages, bring hero and heroine together, perform services for their friends, and resolve quarrels. As with the group leaders of Chapter Six, Rūpa says there are twelve varieties of friend.[38]

In the rest of Chapter Eight, Rūpa takes up the role of friends as messengers (*dūtya*). He divides friends into five categories. The first is the perpetual heroine (*nitya-nāyikā*). She is the group leader and within her group, she is the absolute most fortunate (*ātyantikādhikā*). Though she is a friend, she never acts as a messenger for her friends in her group. Second beneath her is the heroine for the most part (*nāyikā-prāya*). She is relatively more fortunate and a heroine with respect to those beneath her, a friend and messenger for her group leader. The third is the relatively equal messenger-friend. She is a messenger-friend for those above her and a heroine-friend for those beneath her. The fourth, who is relatively minimal in fortune, is a messenger-friend for the most part (*sakhī-prāya*). She is a messenger-friend for those above her and a heroine-friend for those beneath her, but occasionally out of their love for her she is a heroine-friend among those above her as well. Finally, the last is the absolute least fortunate friend. She is the perpetual friend (*nitya-sakhī*) and messenger-friend for all, but never a heroine-friend. Rūpa concludes with a discussion of the different levels of affection of the friends towards their group leaders and Kṛṣṇa. Some have more affection for Kṛṣṇa than for their group leaders. Some have equal affection for both. And some have more affection for their group

---

[38] See the previous footnote.

leader than for Kṛṣṇa.

Chapter Nine, which has fifty-three stanzas, completes Rūpa's discussion of the ladies of Vraja by turning our attention to their relationships with one another, both within their own groups and with ladies in other groups. Rūpa organizes this chapter around four types of ladies, depending on their attitudes toward self and others. His first type of lady is self-promoting; the second type promotes her friends. The third type is indifferent to relative status; and the fourth type acts aggressively against others. This chapter ends Rūpa's treatment of the subjective supporting stimulants (*ālambana-vibhāva*) first outlined in Chapter Three. So, too, ends the discussion of the subclass of supporting stimulants as subject (*āśraya-ālambana-vibhāva*) which refers, in this sacred erotic rapture, to the village ladies of Vraja.

In Chapter Ten, which has one hundred and ten stanzas, Rūpa describes another kind of stimulant called the illuminating stimulant (*uddīpana-vibhāva*). This refers to elements of dramatic and poetic representation such as place, time, and situation, as well as to the attractive qualities of the lovers (Kṛṣṇa and the ladies of Vraja), their various names, characters, ornaments, things related to them (footprints, for instance), and external elements like descriptions of nature, the seasons, forests, night, the moon, and so forth. These are all the elements that would evoke or excite feelings of love in the hero and heroine and by extension in sensitive audience members. Attractive qualities, for instance, are divided into three types: physical, mental, and verbal. Some examples of attractive mental qualities are gratefulness, patience, compassion, and such. Examples of attractive verbal qualities are using words in ways that are pleasing to the ear, and so forth. Physical qualities are youth, beauty, complexion, sweetness, softness, and so forth. Chapter Ten contains a wealth of stanzas to trigger the *bhakti-rasa* response.

In Chapter Eleven, which has one hundred and five stanzas, we find descriptions of the consequents (*anubhāva*), the outward signs of the inner emotional state, delight in Kṛṣṇa (*kṛṣṇa-rati*), which is evoked by the illuminating stimulants described in Chapter Ten. These are of three types: the "ornaments" (*alaṅkāra*, twenty-two of them), the "shining ones" (*udbhāsvara*, seven), and the "verbal ones" (*vācika*, twelve). Among the ornaments there are physical (three), effortless (seven), and natural (twelve). To give a brief example of the only first group of three physical ornaments, the first, called *bhāva*, is the first turning of a placid, unruffled mind toward love. The second, called *hāva*, is "the call" to love indicated by a lady's bend of the neck, a widening of her eyes and brows, small, subtle signs of love's first arrival. The third physical ornament, called *helā*, produces clear signs of physical excitement, heavy breathing, goosebumps, a loosening of clothes, and so forth. In this chapter, as with all the rest, each type of consequent, is an opportunity for Rūpa to compose a poem or to cite a suitable poem from another work, and a chance for readers to taste sacred rapture.

Chapter Twelve, which has thirty-eight stanzas, introduces another kind of consequent called *sāttvika-bhāvas*, translated here as "autonomic physical reactions or consequents" (*sāttvika-bhāva*). There are eight of these: paralysis, perspiration, goose-bumps, cracking of the voice, trembling, discoloration, tears, and fainting. These, when enacted in plays or skillfully portrayed in poetry as belonging to the characters, strengthen the power of the work of art to evoke sacred rapture in the audience. In addition, those who have sufficiently developed their memory traces through religious practice, as discussed before, may manifest these autonomous reactions themselves as members of the audience who also taste sacred rapture. According to Rūpa, there are four levels of increasing manifestation of these reactions: smoldering, burning, burning brightly, and blazing up.

Chapter Thirteen, which has one hundred and ten stanzas, contains descriptions of the various transitory emotions (*vyabhicāri-bhāvas*) that appear and disappear in the course of the development of love between Kṛṣṇa and the village ladies. They are said to rise up out of the enduring emotion like waves out of the ocean, increasing its size and power briefly and then merging back into it.[39] All the thirty-three transitory emotions, except for wrathfulness (*ugratā*) and apathy (*ālasya*), can appear as enhancements of the sweet rapture (*madhura-rasa*) in Rūpa's treatment. Sometimes several transitory emotions arise at the same time. Thus, towards the end of this chapter Rūpa discusses the interactions of these transitory emotions with each other. They arise at various points, connect with each other, mix together, and then resove into tranquility.

The next two chapters (fourteen and fifteen) are in many ways the core of the text. In terms of the number of stanzas in them, just the two of them account for about a third (491 out of 1451) of the stan-

[39]Rūpa, ONSR, 2.4.3. The metaphor of ocean and waves ultimately derives from the *Nāṭya-śāstra* (75-83).

zas of the whole text. The fourteenth chapter is about the enduring emotion, sweet delight in Kṛṣṇa (*madhurā kṛṣṇa-rati*). The fifteenth is about sacred erotic rapture (*madhura-rasa or śṛṅgāra-rasa*). These two are specially long because of the complexity and centality of the subject matter. We have already talked about the rise (like a ray of sunlight) of the generic or basic enduring emotion in the heart or mind of the *bhakta* on the basis of Rūpa's previous work the *Ocean of the Nectar of Sacred Rapture*. The enduring emotion there is initially described as delignt in Kṛṣṇa (*kṛṣṇa-rati*). That enduring emotion has five types or flavors and among those five types the final one, sweet delight in Kṛṣṇa, Rūpa considers to be the best in terms of the intensity of the special pleasure it provides.

In Chapter Fourteen Rūpa describes the causes and various advanced conditions of sweet delight in Kṛṣṇa (*madhura-kṛṣṇa-rati*). Beginning with the various ways in which it arises, he goes on to describe and exemplify in detail its advanced levels of development. The ways in which sweet delight in Kṛṣṇa arises are: by encounter (*abhiyoga*), through the sense objects (*viṣaya*, i.e. sound, touch, sight, taste, and fragrance), by connection or relationship (*sambandha*, family, etc.), through self-assurance (*abhimāna*, perhaps more aptly understood as stubbornness), through something specific to him (his footprints, for instance), through something or someone resembling him, and by one's own nature. As with many of Rūpa's lists these are organized in hierarchical order, from the least preferred to the most. The arising of sweet delight in Kṛṣṇa by one's own nature is the highest and occurs only among the ladies of Vraja.

Delight in Kṛṣṇa once it has manifested has, according to Rūpa, three major varieties: common or ordinary (*sādhāraṇī*), proper or virtuous (*samañjasā*), and powerful or overwhelming (*samarthā*). Common delight in Kṛṣṇa is exemplified by Kubjā whose love for Kṛṣṇa is sudden and not very deep. It arose on meeting him personally during his visit to Mathurā and was aimed primarily at achieving her own pleasure. Her affair with Kṛṣṇa is described in the Tenth Skandha of the *Bhāgavata Purāṇa*.[40] Virtuous delight in Kṛṣṇa is that felt by his wives in Dvārakā or by those who regard themselves as his wives. It is born by hearing of his virtues, deeds, and character and in other indirect ways. Though it is strong, it is sometimes divided by the desire for one's own

[40]Bhāg. 10.42.1-14.

pleasure. In powerful delight in Kṛṣṇa, however, the desire for one's own pleasure has been absorbed into itself by delight in Kṛṣṇa which itself has become somewhat distinct and more powerful. One's own pleasure becomes one with the pleasing of Kṛṣṇa. Thus, the desire for one's own pleasure does not divide it any more. It is born from the lover's own nature and from even the slightest connection with Kṛṣṇa (i.e., from merely hearing his name) and it is so strong that it causes all other attachments, attractions, and identifications to be forgotten. It is found only among the fortunate ladies of Vraja.

In the rest of the chapter, Rūpa gives a detailed account of the higher stages of the enduring emotion, delight in Kṛṣṇa. These stages develop in the following order: divine love for Kṛṣṇa (*preman*), deep affection (*sneha*), a kind of feigned haughtiness or pride (*māna*, to disguise the excessive inner melting of one's heart because of affection), loving confidence (*praṇaya*, considering oneself not different from one's beloved), passion (*rāga*, when even great pain is perceived as happines in one's mind), deep attachment (*anurāga*, when one's beloved seems ever newer and fresh though seen every day), and finally the grand emotion (*bhāva* or *mahābhāva*, deep attachment at its supreme limit). These each have several varieties which Rūpa defines and for which he gives examples. Rūpa gives, as a metaphor for the stages of delight in Kṛṣṇa, the various stages in the refining of sugar. One starts with the seed (delight in Kṛṣṇa), the sugar cane plant (divine love for Kṛṣṇa), the juice (deep affection), thickened molasses (feigned haughtiness), hardened molasses (loving confidence), brown sugar (passion), white sugar (deep attachment), and rock candy or crystalized candy (the grand emotion).

In Chapter Fifteen we find descriptions and examples of the various expressions of sacred erotic rapture (*śṛṅgāra, madhura, ujjvala-rasa*). To distinguish the subject matter of Chapter 14 from that of Chapter 15 we can appeal to an example as old as Bharata's first treatment of aesthetic rapture in his *Treatise on Drama* (4th cent. CE.). There the metaphor of food is used.[41] The items discussed in Chapter 14 are like the ingredients used in cooking various types of tasteful foods. In this

---

[41]Nś., verse 6.32 and preceding prose passage: *ko dṛṣṭāntaḥ | atrāha—yathā hi nānāvyañjanauṣadhidravyasaṃyogād rasaniṣpattiḥ tathā nānābhāvopagamādrasaniṣpattiḥ*, "What example can be given? Here one says just as by the combination of various vegetables, spices, and substances flavor is produced, so by the combination of various emotions, aesthetic taste is produced."

chapter Rūpa presents the various "flavors" of those "foods" made with the emotional ingredients of Chapter 14.

Sacred erotic rapture is the subject of Chapter 15. It has two major flavors: love-in-separation (*vipralambha*) and love-in-the-enjoyment-of-union (*sambhoga*). When a couple is not together or when they are together but they cannot embrace and show the love they wish to, their feelings for each other become heightened and they are said to be experiencing love-in-separation. Love-in-separation increases the excellence of love-in-union.

There are four types of love-in-separation: prior passion (new love before the first meeting with one's beloved), love quarrel, love-diversity (expressed as fear of future separation while in the presence of one's lover), and separation of the lovers because of near or far trips away. Each of the types of separation are described and the first and the last are given ten stages of increasing intensity. For example, prior passion in its developed form passes through ardent desire, anxiety, sleeplessness, loss of weight, dullness, impulsiveness, illness, madness, fainting, and death. Love quarrel is either caused or uncaused and is overcome by appeasement, gifts, cleverly breaking the anger, and neglect.

Love-in-the-enjoyment-of-union is also of two types: primary and secondary (that is, in dream). Each has four subtypes corresponding to the four types of separation. These are the brief encounter (after prior passion), the mixed encounter (after love quarrel), the accomplished meeting (after returning from a trip to a nearby place), and finally, the exubrant encounter after returning from a distant trip). Rūpa comments that the descriptions of love-in-separation apply only to the manifest sport of Kṛṣṇa in this world. In Kṛṣṇa's eternal sport in the eternal Vṛndāvana he is never separated from the ladies of Vraja.[42]

Kṛṣṇa's Extra-marital Loves?

In defining sacred rapture (*bhakti-rasa*) and turning to the discussion of its various components, Rūpa begins with the stimulants. The first of the stimulants is the hero-lover (*nāyaka*), Kṛṣṇa, and Rūpa distinguishes between Kṛṣṇa's two roles: Kṛṣṇa as married lover and Kṛṣṇa as paramour or extra-marital lover. Each typifies a different quality

[42]Un., 15.185-6.

and intensity of erotic love. Between the two, Rūpa favors the extra-marital type for its rich metaphorical resonances and the intensity of its passion. He hardly discusses married love and gives only a few examples demonstrating it. Extra-marital affairs in ordinary heros are indeed base, but not in Kṛṣṇa. As Rūpa says in the *Blazing Sapphire* (1.21):

> "The baseness that is claimed for this [extra-marital love] only applies to ordinary [human] heroes, not to Kṛṣṇa who has descended [to earth] in order to taste the essence of rapture (*rasa*)."[43]

For Rūpa the essence of sacred rapture is sacred erotic rapture in which the conditions of extra-marital love make passion the most powerful driving force capable of overcoming all obstacles. In defining extra-marital love a few verses earlier (1.17), he says "the rules of accepted moral behavior are transgressed by passion for the wife of another" (*rāgeṇollaṅgayan dharmam parakīyāvalārthinā*). This passion that transgresses social norms and responsibilities supplies a metaphor for how one should love the supreme being, Kṛṣṇa, above all else and at whatever cost or risk.

Kṛṣṇa had many wives according to the mythology (16,108 at his capital city, Dvārakā) and, indeed, a few examples of that type of love are given in Rūpa's text (see stanzas 13-14 in Chapter One). This is the socially acceptable form of love meant to support and promote the "family values" and reigning social structure of ancient and medieval India. Its purpose is primarily procreation, although it certainly has other more playful dimensions, as Rūpa's stanzas demonstrate. It is understood, however, that Kṛṣṇa also loved and was loved by the *gopīs*, the women of the cowherd community in which he grew up, many of whom were married to others. In this transgressive form of love Rūpa finds the real structure of higher divine love. The *gopīs* risk everything for their love of Kṛṣṇa. They were willing to throw everything away for him: their social standing, the respect of their families, their husbands and children, their property and possessions, and even their hope for better lives in future births. They prove the power of their love by

---

[43]Un., 1.21:

> *laghutvam atra yat proktaṃ tat tu prākṛta-nāyake|*
> *na kṛṣṇe rasaniryāsa-svādārtham avatāriṇi||*

turning away from all these things without hesitation. Their love is animated by a passion that surpasses all, and they—the most advanced—the *samarthā nāyikās*—are not interested in their own well-being or happiness. For them, the sexual act is a way of giving everything they have to Kṛṣṇa and giving him as much pleasure as they can without expecting anything from him in return. It is therefore transformed into a selfless act of *bhakti* or *preman*, divine love. This form of sacrifice is technically akin to the old Vedic sacrifices in which something dear is given up and the receiver of the gift is bound by the gift to the giver. In this case, however, the giving is an act of love, not of exchange or business. In the *Bhāgavata Purāṇa* Kṛṣṇa expresses his inability to repay the Vraja ladies for their sacrifices on his behalf. The *gopīs* thus become models for how the true *bhakta* should feel and act towards Kṛṣṇa.

A stanza of the first chapter of the *Blazing Sapphire* is a specially clear example of Kṛṣṇa's extraordinary attractiveness:

> May he whose self is perfect pleasure,
> divine adventure, richest treasure
> of women young in all three worlds—
> May he bring joy to you.
>
> He, whose eyes with their side-glancing
> enchant all hearts like devīs dancing—
> He, whose grey-blue body, glistening
> seems a rain cloud newly swelling—
> He, whose feet eclipse with their gleaming
> the pride of millions of gods of love—
> May Kṛṣṇa bring joy to you.[44]

All other attractions and attachments are overpowered by the attractiveness of Kṛṣṇa. The only proper response is to drop all other duties and responsibilities, all other attachments and relationships and pursue Kṛṣṇa.

Apart from Kṛṣṇa's supreme attractiveness, the nature of attraction itself is such that it is most powerful when it is hidden and its object is not easily gained. Rūpa quotes a stanza from Bharatamuni (4th-5th cents. CE.), the author of the *Treatise on Drama* (*Nāṭya-śāstra*):

> Perfect erotic love is that in which

[44]Un., 1.5.

> obstacles hinder one's way,
> desires must be concealed,
> and access to each other rare.[45]

For Rūpa, the highest expression of sacred erotic rapture (*sṛṅgāra*) arises out of these conditions.

According to Rūpa and his followers, Kṛṣṇa as paramour demonstrates first and foremost his divinity and absolute sovereignty. He is the law-maker who is himself above the laws. There are no law-makers with authority over him. He is not bound by his laws unless he wants to be and sometimes he does want to be, specially when it enhances the quality of love he experiences as indicated in the stanza just quoted. His transcendence and power are demonstrated by his ability to transgress all boundaries without danger to himself or incurring bad results. In this way Kṛṣṇa is differentiated from all others; he is not to be imitated, cannot be imitated. Rūpa warns us in his *Blazing Sapphire* against imitating Kṛṣṇa. He says (3.24,26):

> Those wishing for their own well being
> should conduct themselves like *bhaktas*,
> but never ever like Kṛṣṇa;
> such has been the full determination
> of the meaning of the texts on *bhakti*.[46]
>
> One who does not have such power
> should never try this even in his mind;

---

[45]Un., 1.20:

> *bahu vāryate khalu yatra pracchannakāmukatvaṃ ca |*
> *yā ca mitho durlabhatā sā manmathasya paramā ratiḥ ||*

This verse in this form does not appear in modern versions of the *Nāṭya-śāstra*. The closest and most likely source of Rūpa's citation is (24.205cd,206):

> *pracchannakāmitvaṃ yattu tadvai ratikaraṃ bhavet ||*
> *yadvāmābhiniveśitvaṃ yataśca vinivāryate |*
> *durlabhatvañca yannāryāḥ sā kāmasya parā ratiḥ ||*

But that hidden desire may be indeed a cause of attraction. Moreover intentness on a woman from whom one is barred and a woman's being difficult to meet are the highest attraction.

[46]Un., 3.24:

> *vartitavyaṃ śamicchadbhir bhaktavan na tu kṛṣṇavat |*
> *ity eva bhaktiśāstrāṇāṃ tātparyasya vinirṇayaḥ ||*

since anyone besides Rudra is killed
who foolishly drinks ocean-born poison.[47]

That is, one should not try to do what Kṛṣṇa has done with the cowherd girls. "Ocean-born poison" is a reference to the Purāṇic myth of the creation of ambrosia and its counterpart, poison, out of the churning of the ocean of milk by the gods and demons. Rudra or Śiva agreed to take the poison into his throat and hold it in order to prevent its harming others. He could do this because of his great power. Others would have died. He is not a model for us like the *gopīs* are. On the other hand, it is the transgressive activities of the Lord, specially in his dealings with the pastoral ladies (*gopī*), that wake us up to the vast gulf of difference between him and us. As the more theologically inclined members of the tradition point out, there is an illusion in the notion of Kṛṣṇa as paramour. Everything, after all, belongs to him. Thus, all the cowherd village ladies (*gopī*) are ultimately his alone; their belonging to others in marriage is the result of worldly illusion. In other words, this tradition has found a way to admire and value Kṛṣṇa's "immoral" actions while yet maintaining a strict demand for morality in its followers.

As refinements of the two major divisions of the lover-hero, married and paramour, Rūpa adopts the standard categories of classical dramatic criticism: noble, playful, peaceful, and haughty. Each of these is considered resolute or self-possessed (*dhīra*). Thus their names are resolute and noble, resolute and playful, resolute and peaceful, and resolute and haughty. This categorization has many interesting features about it. That all are considered resolute points to the fact that classical literary criticism liked heros who were not common or ordinary but elevated, noble, men whom society can look up to. This way of categorizing hero-lovers goes back to the the *Treatise on Drama*, (*Nāṭya-śāstra*). There, each type was associated with a particular sort of character: the haughty were the gods (*deva*), the noble were ministers and commanders, the playful were royal, and the peaceful were brahmins and merchants.[48] A later text on drama the *Daśarūpaka* of

---

[47]Un., 3.26:

naitatsamācarejjātu manasāpi hyanīśvaraḥ |
vinaśyatyācaranmauḍhyādyathārudro 'bdhijaṃ viṣam ||

[48]*Nāṭya-śāstra*, 34.17-21.

Dhanañjaya (9th cent. CE.) reaffirms these categories, though its commentator Dhanika (10th-11th cents. CE.) suggests that these are not really types, but conditions. Thus a hero-lover might at different times be of a different type. Dhanika recommends, however, that in a single work the primary hero be of only one type.[49]

In his previous work, *The Ocean of the Nectar of Sacred Rapture*, Rūpa applies a set of qualities for each of the heros mentioned above, following to a large extent the characterizations of the earlier tradition of literary criticism. Though much more complex than this, the major traits are as follows: the noble one is magnanimous, the playful one is carefree, the peaceful one impartial, and the haughty one is self-centered. Rūpa further sub-divides each of the four main categories into four states or conditions: faithful, courteous, deceitful, and shameless. These characterizations had appeared for the first time in Dhanañjaya's (9th cent.) *Daśarūpaka*. The faithful loves only one lady, the courteous is equal towards many women or, as Rūpa puts it, continues to show affection to one lady while in love with another, the deceitful carries on secretly with other women, and the shameless is brazen about carrying on with other women. The interesting thing about all of this is that, according to Rūpa, Kṛṣṇa can be all of them, even the most despicable. All forms of erotic love have their roots in Kṛṣṇa.

The debate over whether Kṛṣṇa's relationship with Rādhā and the other village ladies is extramarital or marital has occupied the Caitanya tradition almost since its inception in the 16th century. It seems to have flared up at least once a century since then. One might argue that the tradition from its beginning has been bifurcated into two camps and into two sets of scriptural traditions. The greatest writers of the tradition can be divided into these two camps. The staunchest advocate of the marital interpretation (*svīyatā*) is none other than Rūpa's own nephew, editor, commentator, and the tradition's most accomplished theologian, Jīva Gosvāmin.[50] On the other side of the question one finds Rūpa himself and all the greatest poets of the tradition, Kavi Karṇapūra, Kṛṣṇadāsa Kavirāja, Viśvanātha Cakravartin, and many of

---

[49]Dhanañjaya, *Daśarūpaka*, 2.3-6.

[50]See Jan Brzezinski's excellent account of Jīva's arguments in favor of the village women (*gopīs*) being Kṛṣṇa's wives in his article entitled "Does Kṛṣṇa Marry the Gopīs in the End?," in the *Journal of Vaiṣṇava Studies* (vol. 5, no. 4, Fall 1997), 49-110. Sadly, he treats the extra-marital side only briefly.

the writers of Bengali songs.

To an impartial observer, it would appear that both sides are right in their own ways. Each side approaches the question from a different perspective. Jīva and those who follow him employ a theological perspective: Kṛṣṇa is the supreme being and all beings and all things properly belong to him. There is no other to compete with or limit him. Any appearance to the contrary is an illusion and this is Jīva's point: the appearance of the village women's being married to other men and having children by them is an illusion. This is a teaching as old as the Upaniṣads, in particular the *Īśopaniṣad* (500-400 BCE). The first mantra of the Upaniṣad is:

> Oṁ. All this is inhabited [owned] by the Lord,
> Whatever moves in the world of motion.
> Enjoy only that which is set aside by him [for you];
> Don't steal anyone's property.[51]

Not satisfied with this generic "belonging" to Kṛṣṇa, however, Jīva claims that there was an actual marriage between Kṛṣṇa and the ladies of Vraja. Kṛṣṇa returns to Vraja and marries the village ladies after being informed by Paurṇamāsī that their marriages to other cowherds were illusions. Such a return to Vraja is not mentioned in the *Bhāgavata Purāṇa* which is the primary authoritative account of the life of Kṛṣṇa for the Caitanya tradition, though that tradition has had no qualms about adding to and embellishing that story in its many literary works. Nevertheless, Jīva, in his master work, the *Life of Gopāla (Kṛṣṇa)* (*Gopāla-campū*), describes their marriage.[52]

The proponents of the extra-marital position do not disagree with Jīva's theological reading. They, however, approach the question from the point of view of sacred rapture and argue that sacred erotic rapture is heightened and intensified when it appears to be extra-marital. Though the Vraja ladies may be, in theological terms, the powers or *śaktis* of Kṛṣṇa, their love for Kṛṣṇa is sweetened when they and he

---

[51] *Īśopaniṣad Upaniṣad*, 1:

> *oṁ īśāvāsyamidaṁ sarvaṃ*
> *yatkiṃca jagatyāṃ jagat |*
> *tena tyaktena bhuñjīthā*
> *mā gṛdhaḥ kasya sviddhanam ||1||*

My translation.

[52] Jīva Gosvāmin, *Life of Gopāla*, 1.33.

believe they are not connected by marriage, but by a passion that disregards social and religious rules and regulations. This seems to be the intent of Rūpa's teaching in his *Blazing Sapphire*. It is certainly the position defended by Rūpa's second major commentator, Viśvanātha Cakravartin (17th cent.).

Plagiarism? Rūpa's Use of Siṃhabhūpāla

In studying Rūpa's *Blazing Sapphire* closely I began to realize that though he drew from a number of previous writers, he drew more heavily from one particular writer, a learned, literary king from South India named Siṃhabhūpāla II (1381 CE). The center of his power was the town of Recharla in Andhra, very close to its border with Karnatak.[53] Siṃhabhūpāla's work on drama and poetry is called the *Moon of the Ocean of Rapture* (*Rasārṇava-sudhākara*). That Rūpa occasionally quoted from Siṃhabhūpāla's work has been known for some time. S.K. De in his work on Caitanya Vaiṣṇavism, *Early History of the Vaiṣṇava Faith and Movement in Bengal*, says that Rūpa quotes Siṃhabhūpāla once in his *Ocean of the Nectar of Sacred Rapture* and five times in his *Blazing Sapphire* (5.25, 10.41, 10.59, 10.64, 10.101).[54] De also points out several places where Rūpa follows the system laid out by Siṃhabhūpāla.

In all of the places where Rūpa uses example stanzas from Siṃhabhūpāla he cites them as *Rasasudhākare*, "in the *Moon of Rasa*." However, during my work on Rūpa's text, I have noticed that Rūpa will often use Siṃhabhūpāla's words—exactly or with small variations—when defining many of his technical terms. He does so then without mentioning their source as Siṃhabhūpāla. I have footnoted this source whenever a borrowing occurs in the selections presented here. By today's standards these would be considered plagiarisms. However, it would be unfair to apply today's standards and practices to ancient and medieval India. I can imagine alternative ways of thinking of Rūpa's unaccredited borrowings.

One can suggest, for instance, that Rūpa, when he borrowed from Siṃhabhūpāla's definitions or significant parts of them, expected his

---

[53]Siṃhabhūpāla II, *The Rasārṇavasudhākara of Siṃhabhūpāla*, edited by T. Venkatacharya. (Adyar, Madras: The Adyar Library and Reseach Center, 1979)

[54]S.K. De, *Early History of the Vaiṣṇava Faith and Movement in Bengal*, 202, 221. (Calcutta: Firma KLM Private Limited, Repr. 1986)

audience to be educated in much the same way he had been. His audience, therefore, would certainly recognize Rūpa's definitions as affirmations or adaptations of those of Siṃhabhūpāla, not definitions he had come up with on his own. On the other hand, when it came to the example stanzas, those could have been from any number of sources and authors. Thus, when Rūpa cites Siṃhabhūpāla's example stanzas, he recognizes them as Siṃhabhūpāla's work. Furthermore, Rūpa's lack of strict recognition of his sources in didactic verses need not be interpreted as plagiarism because there is a sense among traditional writers in India that if someone has already defined a term well, it is foolish and even disrespectful to that writer, who can be regarded as one's teacher or guru, to try to improve on it. On the other hand, if a definition is determined to be flawed, it is a writer's responsibility, while recognizing one's indebtedness to that writer, to try to improve it.

One can draw the further, and more interesting, conclusion that when it comes to the discussion of *rasa* in drama and poetry, Rūpa preferred Siṃhabhūpāla's presentation to Viśvanātha Kavirāja's (14-15th cent. CE.) in his *Mirror of Literature* (*Sāhitya-darpaṇa*). Siṃhabhūpāla represents the southern Indian tradition of *rasa* aesthetics coming from Bhojarāja of Malwar (10-11th cents. CE.) whereas the work of Viśvanātha Kavirāja represents the northern tradition of *rasa* aesthetics coming from Abhinavagupta. There are significant differences between the northern and southern traditions.[55]

This Collection of Poems

This book is the first volume of a selection of Rūpa's most delightful poems from his *Blazing Sapphire*. It covers only the first seven chapters of the text with annotations from the major commentaries and introductory hints about who is speaking and why. Translations of selected poems from the rest of the chapters of the *Blazing Sapphire* will appear in volumes two (chapters 8-13) and three (chapters 14-15). In the first seven chapters there are a total of four hundred and seven stanzas out of which we have included around one hundred. We have focused almost entirely on the example poems, leaving the didactic verses aside,

[55]See my dissertation on the subject, *Sacred Rapture: A Study of the Religious Aesthetic of Śrī Rūpa Gosvāmin*, University of Chicago, 1990. Partially available online at http://www.caitanya-symposium.org/Sacred-rapture-master.pdf

except when they are necessary for understanding the example poems. Then, for the most part, the didactic verses are placed in footnotes along with translations.

The original Sanskrit texts of the poems are provided on the left hand pages facing their translations on the right hand pages. The texts are given both in the Sanskrit script called *devanāgarī* ("city of the gods") and in the standard transliteration system for the English alphabet. In an appendix a pronunciation guide is given for the sounds of the Sanskrit alphabet as well as a guide matching the Sanskrit letters with their Roman transliterations. In addition, the Sanskrit conjuncts—in which several letters are joined together into forms that often look quite different from their components—are shown with their Roman equivalents. Finally, there is a bibliography including the main texts used for this translation and introduction.

Shortly after this abridged translation, the first volume of a complete multivolume translation of the *Blazing Sapphire* will appear. The first volume, entitled "Kṛṣṇa and his Friends" will contain all the verses of chapters one and two in bilingual format. It will include three of the four traditional Sanskrit commentaries in appendices. Other volumes will appear periodically until the work is complete.

I have used five editions for this text and translation. The one that has been almost inseparable from me over the years of my study of the *Blazing Sapphire* is the Vrajajīvan Prācyabhāratī Granthamālā no. 2 edition of the *Ujjvala-nīlamaṇi* with the commentaries of Jīva Gosvāmin and Viśvanātha Cakravartin (Delhi: Chaukhamba Sanskrit Pratisthan, 1985). This is really a reprint of the 1932 edition of volume 95 of the Kāvyamālā Series (Bombay: Nirnaya Sagar Press, 1932). The edition of the *Ujjvala-nīlamaṇi* in the Bengali script by Rāmanārāyaṇa Vidyāratna (Murshidabad: Rādhāramaṇa Press of Baharampura, 1304 BS [1898 CE]) also with the commentaries of Jīva and Viśvanātha, has been useful for comparison purposes when the readings of the Kāvyamālā edition seemed problematic or suspect. This edition also has a good Bengali translation accompanying the text. Another edition I made use of is that of Haridāsa Dāsa Bābā (Navadvīp, Bengal: Haribol Kuṭira, 478 GA [1964 CE]) in Bengali script with a commentary by Viṣṇudāsa Gosvāmin, a disciple of Kṛṣṇadāsa Kavirāja. It also contains a good Bengali translation with the text. Another useful edition of the text is that published by Kṛṣṇadāsa Bābā (Kusumasarovara: Kṛṣṇadāsabābā, Samvat 2022 [1965 CE]). It contains no commentaries, but has a Hindi introduction and translation along with the text. Finally, I had access to a photocopy of the superb edition by Puridāsa in Bengali script (Vṛndāvanadhāma: Haridāsa Śarma, 1954) with the commentaries of Jīva and Viśvanātha. This last edition contains a number of variant readings from two of the editions mentioned above (Kāvyamālā and Murshidabad) and from four manuscripts from libraries in Bengal and Orissa.

Conclusion

The poetry of the *Blazing Sapphire* operates on a number of levels. In the first place it is simply beautiful Sanskrit poetry either written or chosen by one of the 16th century's master poets. Unfortunately, much of that richness and beauty, the sound and rhythms, the astonishing double entendre, the emotional depth and sweetness, is lost in the translation of the stanzas into English. There is ultimately no substitute for reading them in Sanskrit. (That's why the original Sanskrit stanzas are included across from their translations.) However, a little something of the originals can be carried over into their English versions if one is clever enough. I thank my wife, Elizabeth, for helping me with that aspect of the translations, taking my rather clunky, far too literal English versions and restoring to them a fraction of the beauty, rhythm, and life of the Sanskrit originals.

In the second place, the jewel-like stanzas of the *Sapphire* come within the long and brilliant tradition of India's *rasa* aesthetics. Evoking or inducing *rasa* is one of the major purposes for which they were written. In Rūpa's hands the stanzas were aimed in the direction of sacred rapture (*bhakti-rasa*), the core of the fundamental religious experience of his tradition, without closing off the possibility of readers having a purely aesthetic experience. For those who see nothing special in Kṛṣṇa, the stanzas are still accessible vehicles of aesthetic delight. The *rasa* aesthetic is one of India's brilliant gifts to the world and whether or not one is able to taste *rasa*, exposure to a discussion of the theory is an invaluable expansion of one's liberal education. It should help deepen one's experience not only of the literature of India, but of all literature no matter where it was produced.

Finally, there is the wisdom of the stanzas which comes from Rūpa's poetic vision and the tradition he belonged to. By wisdom I mean the beautiful view of the world that can be glimpsed through these stanzas, a view in which the divine and the human world commingle, in which unselfish love emerges as the primary goal of life, and in which unity and diversity, the one and the many, blend together in incomprehensible ways allowing neither to devour or eclipse the other. All the objects of this world, on the one hand, are part of, and point beyond themselves to, a larger inclusive reality into which everything fits. On the other hand, that all-encompassing reality reveals its vast diversity in all the beings and things that we are, but often fail to recognize. Rūpa's view is vibratory in nature moving back and forth from love-in-separation to love-in-union. The first intensifies the second and the second enriches the first. Together they keep on growing and growing and the glue that holds them together is Kṛṣṇa, whether he is absent or present. The force that runs through these vibrational waves is Rādhā or love.

Part I

Text and Translation

Chapter One: Varieties of the Hero

Kṛṣṇa's Dance of Delight (*Rāsa-līlā*)

नामाकृष्टरसज्ञः शीलेनोद्दीपयन् सदानन्दम् ।
निजरूपोत्सवदायी सनातनात्मा प्रभुर्जयति ॥ १ ॥

nāmākṛṣṭarasajñaḥ śīlenoddīpayan sadānandam |
nijarūpotsavadāyī sanātanātmā prabhurjayati ||1||

Glory to the eternal Lord[1]
Whose name attracts those who know rapture.[2]
His character always excites Nanda,[3]
Giver of the joy of his own beauty.

(or)

Glory to the Master,[4] who is
The very self of my Sanātana.[5]
His tongue repeats the holy name,
His character ever delights the good,
And he gives joy to his Rūpa.[6]

(or)

Glory to my guide in Sanātana,[7]
Whose tongue repeats the holy name.
His character ever delights the good,
And he gives joy to his Rūpa.[8] (1)

---

[1]That is, to Śrī Kṛṣṇa. This verse is an example of poetic pun or double-entendre. The same verse is meant to be interpreted in at least three different ways, that is, as indicating three different people, by reading its words in three different ways. The technical term for this in Sanskrit literary theory is *śleṣa* or "embrace." Three different meanings embrace this one set of words. In order to demonstrate those three meanings, I have given three translations of this verse. Rūpa has succeeded in offering praise to Lord Kṛṣṇa, his *guru* Caitanya, and his older brother Sanātana who was also his mentor.

[2]*Rasa,* or *bhakti-rasa,* sometimes translated as aesthetic rapture and sacred rapture, respectively.

[3]Nanda, leader of the cowherders of Vraja, who believes he is Kṛṣṇa's father.

[4]In this case, to Śrī Caitanya

[5]Sanātana Gosvāmin, the author Rūpa's elder brother and mentor.

[6]The author, Rūpa Gosvāmin. This could also be taken as before: "Giver of the joy of his own beauty."

[7]Again Rūpa's older brother.

[8]Un., 1.1

मुख्यरसेषु पुरा यः संक्षेपेणोदितो रहस्यत्वात् ।
पृथगेव भक्तिरसराट् स विस्तरेणोच्यते मधुरः ॥२॥

mukhyaraseṣu purā yaḥ saṃkṣepeṇodito rahasyatvāt |
pṛthageva bhaktirasarāṭ sa vistareṇocyate madhuraḥ ||2||

Since it's secret among major raptures,
It was discussed only briefly before.[9]
Madhura,[10] the king of sacred raptures,
We describe in depth by itself. (2)

[9]Un., 1.2. In his previous work, *The Ocean of the Nectar of Sacred Rapture* (*Bhakti-rasāmṛta-sindhu*), Rūpa gives the following reasons for not expanding on this form of sacred rapture in that book (3.5.2):

nivṛttānupayogitvāddurūhatvādayaṃ rasaḥ|
rahasyatvācca saṃkṣipya vitatāṅgo'pi likhyate

"Because it is not suitable for the renounced, because it is hard to understand, and because it is esoteric, this rapture is only briefly described here, though it is vast."

[10]The "sweet" sacred rapture (*bhakti-rasa*), that is, the erotic sacred rapture.

वक्ष्यमाणैर्विभावाद्यैः स्वाद्यतां मधुरा रतिः ।
नीता भक्तिरसः प्रोक्तो मधुराख्यो मनीषिभिः ॥ ३ ॥

vakṣyamāṇairvibhāvādyaiḥ svādyatāṃ madhurā ratiḥ |
nītā bhaktirasaḥ prokto madhurākhyo manīṣibhiḥ ||3||

Sweet erotic love, when tasted
by means of verbal signs and the rest—[11]
as shall soon be described—
Becomes the sacred rapture
the wise call "the sweet one."[12] (3)

[11]These are the stimulants (*vibhāva*, also translated as "determinants" or "excitants"), the consequents or reactions (*anubhāva*), and the transitory emotions (*vyabhicāri-bhāvas*) which when combined cause or suggest an enduring emotion (*sthāyi-bhāva*). The emotion that is evoked by the stimulants is "tasted" or experienced as *rasa* or rapture, according to Bharata's *Nāṭya-śāstra* (6.32).

na hi rasād ṛte kaścid arthaḥ pravartate |
tatra vibhāvānubhāvavyabhicārisaṃyogād rasaniṣpattiḥ |

"Without *rasa* (enjoyment, pleasure, aesthetic rapture) no meaning or value arises. In this matter, from the combination of stimulants, reactions, and transitory emotions, *rasa* is produced."

In Rūpa's adaption of aesthetic rapture to sacred rapture (*bhakti-rasa*) the same general principles apply as he says in his previous book, *The Ocean of the Nectar of Sacred Rapture* (*Bhakti-rasāmṛta-sindhu*) (2.1.5):

vibhāvair anubhāvaiś ca sāttvikairvyabhicāribhiḥ |
svādyatvaṃ hṛdi bhaktānām ānitā śravaṇādibhiḥ |
eṣā kṛṣṇaratiḥ sthāyibhāvo bhaktiraso bhavet ||

"This enduring emotion, love for Kṛṣṇa, becomes sacred rapture, when led to the state of being enjoyed in the hearts of *bhaktas* by the stimulants, consequents, and transitory emotions through hearing, and other kinds of *bhakti*." Future references to this book will be abbreviated Brs. or ONSR. See the introduction for a more detailed account of the production or evocation of *rasa*.

[12]Un., 1.3.

तत्र विभावेष्वालम्बनाः
अस्मिन्नालम्बनाः प्रोक्ताः कृष्णस्तस्य च वल्लभाः ॥ ४॥

tatra vibhāveṣvālambanāḥ
asminnālambanāḥ proktāḥ kṛṣṇastasya ca vallabhāḥ || 4||

Among the stimulants are the supports:

Kṛṣṇa and the women he loves
are called "supports"[13] of this rapture.[14] (4)

[13]The stimulants or *vibhāvas* are divided into two types, supports (*ālambana*) and illuminants (*uddīpana*). Here the support type (*ālambana-vibhāva*) of this rapture is described. Rūpa says in his earlier work (Brs. 2.14,16,273,301,2.21-2):

tatra jñeyā vibhāvāstu ratyāsvādanahetavaḥ|
te dvidhālambanā eke tathaivoddīpanāḥ pare||
kṛṣṇaśca kṛṣṇabhaktāśca budhairālambanā matāḥ|
ratyādervişayatvena tathādhāratayāpi ca||
tadbhāvabhāvitasvāntāḥ kṛṣṇabhaktā itīritāḥ||
uddīpanāstu te proktā bhāvamuddīpayanti ye|
te tu kṛṣṇacandrasya guṇāścеṣṭāḥ prasādhanam||

"Here it is to be known that the stimulants (*vibhāvas*) are the causes of the tasting of love (*rati*) and the other enduring emotions. They are of two kinds: some are supports (*ālambana*) and others excitants or illuminants (*uddīpana*). Kṛṣṇa and his *bhaktas* are considered supports by the wise, either as the objects of that love or as the possessors or vessels of that love. Those whose hearts of infused with feelings for him are Kṛṣṇa's *bhaktas*. The illuminants are Kṛṣṇa's qualities, actions, and embellishments that excite or illuminate the enduring emotions." Rūpa's discussion of the support variety of stimulant extends over the first nine chapters of this book. In the tenth chapter he takes up the illuminant (*uddīpana*) variety of stimulant.

[14]Un., 1.4.

तत्र कृष्णो यथा

पदद्युतिविनिर्धुतस्मरपरार्धरूपोद्धतिर्
दृगञ्चलकलानटीपटिमभिर्मनोमोहिनी ।
स्फुरन्नवघनाकृतिः परमदिव्यलीलानिधिः
क्रियात्तव जगत्त्रयीयुवतिभाग्यसिद्धिर्मुदम् ॥५॥

tatra kṛṣṇo yathā

padadyutivinirdhutasmaraparārdharūpoddhatir
dṛgañcalakalānaṭīpaṭimabhirmanomohinī |
sphurannavaghanākṛtiḥ paramadivyalīlānidhiḥ
kriyāttava jagattrayīyuvatibhāgyasiddhirmudam ||*5*||

Kṛṣṇa as supporting stimulant:

[*This is Paurṇamāsī's blessing for Rādhā.* (V)]

May he whose self is perfect pleasure,
divine adventure, richest treasure
of women young in all three worlds—
May he bring joy to you.

He, whose eyes with their side-glancing
enchant all hearts like devīs dancing—
He, whose grey-blue body, glistening
seems a rain cloud newly swelling—
He, whose feet eclipse with their gleaming
the pride of millions of gods of love—
May Kṛṣṇa bring joy to you.[15] (5)

[15]Un., 1.5. This is a blessing given by the elder lady Pūrṇamāsī to Rādhā who was bowing to her in a state of prior passion (*pūrva-rāga*) for Kṛṣṇa, that is, the passion Rādhā felt him before their first meeting. From the commentary of Viśvanātha Cakravartin, hereafter abbreviated as (V).

अयं सुरम्यो मधुरः सर्वसल्लक्षणान्वितः ।
वलीयान्नवतारुण्यो वावदूकः प्रियंवदः ॥६॥

सुधीः सप्रतिभो धीरो विदग्धश्चतुरः सुखी ।
कृतज्ञो दक्षिणः प्रेमवश्यो गम्भीराम्बुधिः ॥७॥

वरीयान् कीर्तिमान् नारीमोहनो नित्यनूतनः ।
अतुल्यकेलिसौन्दर्यप्रेष्ठवंशीस्वनाङ्कितः ॥८॥

ayaṃ suramyo madhuraḥ sarvasallakṣaṇānvitaḥ |
valīyānnavatāruṇyo vāvadūkaḥ priyaṃvadaḥ ||6||

sudhīḥ sapratibho dhīro vidagdhaścaturaḥ sukhī |
kṛtajño dakṣiṇaḥ premavaśyo gambhīrāmbudhiḥ ||7||

varīyān kīrtimān nārīmohano nityanūtanaḥ |
atulyakelisaundaryapreṣṭhavaṃśīsvanāṅkitaḥ ||8||

Kṛṣṇa's many attractive qualities:

[*These are didactic verses.*]

He is very handsome, sweet—
All good traits are Hari's—
Strong in his fresh-blooming youth,
Loquacious, tongue like honey.[16] (6)

Steady, wise, intelligent,
Clever, expert, happy,
Skilled and grateful when he loves,
Loves with abandon, yet
    an ocean of solemnity is Hari.[17] (7)

Great repute is part of him;
    loved ones flock to sport with him,
None can play the flute like him,
    captivate the girls like him;
He excels in everything,
    matchless beauty, ever new.[18] (8)

[16]Un., 1.6. Viśvanātha points out that the first five traits are Kṛṣṇa's physical qualities. Loquaciousness and having a tongue like honey are his verbal traits. The remaing fourteen are his mental traits.

[17]Un., 1.7.

[18]Un., 1.8.

यथा वा (भाग. १०.२२.४४)

कात्यायनि महामाये
महायोगिन्यधीश्वरि ।
नन्दगोपसुतं देवि
पतिं मे कुरु ते नमः ॥१४॥

yathā vā (bhāg. 10.22.44)

kātyāyani mahāmāye
mahāyoginyadhīśvari |
nandagopasutaṃ devi
patiṃ me kuru te namaḥ ||14||

Kṛṣṇa as husband:

[*Some of the maidens of Vraja pray:*]

Oh, Kātyāyanī, Wizardess,
Great Mistress, Goddess, Yoginī
Make the son of cowherd Nanda
Be my husband; this I pray.[19] (9)

---

[19]Bhāg. 10.22.4 cited at Un., 1.14. Rūpa mentions in the next two verses of his work that he heard it said that a text called the *Fundamental Greatness of Mādhava* claimed that before Kṛṣṇa had married Rukmiṇī, his queen in Dvāraka, he had married the girls of Vraja who prayed like this. The text Rūpa mentions has been lost.

यथा पद्यावल्याम् (२०५)

संकेतीकृतकोकिलादिनिनदं कंसद्विषः कुर्वतो
द्वारोन्मोचनलोलशङ्खवलयक्वणं मुहुः शृण्वतः ।
केयं केयमिति प्रगल्भजरतीवाक्येन दूनात्मनो
राधाप्राङ्गणकोणकोलिविटपिक्रोडे गता शर्वरी ॥१८॥

yathā padyāvalyām (205)

saṃketīkṛtakokilādininadaṃ kaṃsadviṣaḥ kurvato
dvāronmocanalolaśaṅkhavalayakvaṇaṃ muhuḥ śṛṇvataḥ |
keyaṃ keyamiti pragalbhajaratīvākyena dūnātmano
rādhāprāṅgaṇakoṇakoliviṭapikroḍe gatā śarvarī ||18||

Kṛṣṇa as paramour:[20]

In the *Garland of Verses* (*Padyāvalī*) (205, by the poet Hara):

[*Vṛndā says this to Paurṇamāsī.* (V)]

Repeatedly he signaled her
By crying the cuckoo's[21] call,
And listened to the jingling
As conch bangle-[adorned arms] opened the door.
But the words of her wily mother-in-law
Jāratī, scorched him:
"Who's this? Who's there?"

The nemisis of Kaṃsa spent that night
In the lap of the jujuba tree
In a corner of Rādhā's courtyard.[22] (10)

---

[20]There are four kinds of husband and four kinds of paramour according to the literary critics Rūpa follows (Siṃhabhūpāla, for instance. See his *The Moon of the Ocean of Rasa* [*Rasārṇava-sudhākara,* hereafter abbreviated as Ras., 1.81]). Rūpa lists them at Un., 1.23:

anukūladakṣiṇaśaṭhā dhṛṣṭaśceti dvayor athocyante|
pratyekaṃ catvāro bhedā yuktibhir amī vṛttyā||

Faithful, courteous, deceitful,
And shameless: these are said to be
The four types of each of the two [husband and lover],
According to reason and behavior.

[21]*Kokila,* the black or Indian cuckoo, whose musical cry is believed to inspire tender emotions.

[22]Un., 1.18.

यथा

वैदग्धीनिकुरम्बचुम्बितधियः सौन्दर्यसारोज्ज्वलाः
कामिन्यः कति नाद्य वल्लवपतेर्दीव्यन्ति गोष्ठान्तरे ।
राधे पुण्यवतीशिखामणिरसि क्षामोदरि त्वां विना
प्रेङ्खन्ती न परासु यन्मधुरिपोर्दृष्टात्र दृष्टिर्या ॥२७॥

yathā

vaidagdhīnikurambacumbitadhiyaḥ saundaryasārojjvalāḥ
kāminyaḥ kati nādya vallavapaterdīvyanti goṣṭhāntare |
rādhe puṇyavatīśikhāmaṇirasi kṣāmodari tvāṃ vinā
preṅkhantī na parāsu yanmadhuripordṛṣṭātra dṛṣṭiryā ||27||

As faithful lover:

[*Vṛndā says this to Rādhā about Kṛṣṇa. (Jīva [J], Viśvanātha [V])*][23]

Are there not, at this moment,
Many lusty and luscious women
Shining in the pastoral village
Of the lord of herdsmen,
Who are ablaze with beauty,
Their minds kissed by many graces?
O slim-waisted Rādhā,
You crown-jewel of virtuous women!
I notice here that the trembling gaze
Of the enemy of Mura[24]
Is only on you, not any other.[25] (11)

[23]Hereafter, Viśvanātha will be abbreviated as (V) and Jīva as (J). See the list of abbreviations on p. xxxviii.
[24]A demon named Mura was defeated by Kṛṣṇa, thus earning him the name Murāri. The story is told in the *Mahābharata, Harivaṃśa,* and the *Bhāgavata Purāṇa* (10.59).
[25]Un., 1.27.

धीरोदात्तानुकूलो यथा

कुवलयदृशः सङ्केतस्था दृगञ्चलकौशलैर्
मनसिजकलानान्दीप्रस्तावनामभितन्वताम् ।
न किल घटते राधारङ्गप्रसङ्गविधायिता-
व्रतविलसिते शैथिल्यस्य च्छटाप्यघविद्विषः ॥२८॥

dhīrodāttānukūlo yathā

kuvalayadṛśaḥ saṅketasthā dṛgañcalakauśalair
manasijakalānāndīprastāvanāmabhitanvatām |
na kila ghaṭate rādhāraṅgaprasaṅgavidhāyitā-
vratavilasite śaithilyasya cchaṭāpyaghavidviṣaḥ ||28||

As resolute and noble faithful lover:[26]

[*Vṛndā says this to a girlfriend of Rādhā. (J) Or, Lalitā, seeing Kṛṣṇa from afar remembering Rādhā, reports this to Citrā. (V)*]

Let all the lotus-eyed ladies
waiting at their trysting places
begin the dramatic prologues
to their playlets on the fine arts
of erotic love. See the skills
of their sidelong glances!
Even this does not cause the Enemy
of Agha to lose interest in the least
in keeping his vow
To gain a role in Rādhā's play.[27] (12)

---

[26]Rūpa describes four subtypes of hero or leading man in his earlier Brs., 2.1.224:

sa punaścaturvidhaḥ syāddhīrodāttaśca dhīralalitaśca |
dhīrapraśāntanāmā tathaiva dhīroddhataḥ kathitaḥ ||

"He again may be of four kinds: resolute and noble, resolute and playful, resolute and peaceful, and resolute and haughty." (Siṃhabhūpāla describes those four at *Rasārṇava-sudhākara*, 1.72b-73a and following.)

Theoretically, Rūpa should provide thirty-two examples for all types of husband and paramour according to these two fourfold classifications (2 x 4 x 4). In actuality he provides examples of the faithful four (resolute and noble faithful, resolute and playful faithful, and so forth), but after that, he does not provide examples of the courteous four, the deceitful four, and the shameless four.

[27]Un., 1.28. Dramatic prologues in Sanskrit dramaturgy give brief, enticing previews of what is to come in the play.

यथा दशरूपके (२.७)

स्नाता तिष्ठति कुन्तलेश्वरसुता वारो ऽङ्गराजस्वसुर्
द्यूते रात्रिरियं जिता कमलया देवी प्रसाद्याद्य च ।
इत्यन्तःपुरसुन्दरीः प्रति मया विज्ञाय विज्ञापिते
देवेनाप्रतिपत्तिमूढमनसा द्वित्राः स्थितं नाडिकाः ॥३५॥

yathā daśarūpake (2.7)

snātā tiṣṭhati kuntaleśvarasutā vāro 'ṅgarājasvasur
dyūte rātririyaṃ jitā kamalayā devī prasādyādya ca |
ityantaḥpurasundarīḥ prati mayā vijñāya vijñāpite
devenāpratipattimūḍhamanasā dvitrāḥ sthitaṃ nāḍikāḥ ||35||

The courteous hero:

[*A messenger, wandering about in the inner chambers of the palace, says this to her friend.*]

"Kuntaleśvara's daughter has been bathed.
It's the turn of Aṅgarāja's sister.
Kamalā won the night at dice,
And Devī wishes to be satisfied."
When thus I informed the wise one
Of the beauties in his harem,
The lord stood still for two or three moments,
Bewildered about what to do.[28] (13)

[28]*Daśa-rūpaka* (2.7) cited at Un., 1.35. This is an example of Kṛṣṇa as the courteous husband.

यथा वा

पद्मा दृग्भङ्गिरलं कलयति कमला जृम्भते साङ्गभङ्गं
तारा दोर्मूलमल्पं प्रथयति कुरुते कर्णकण्डूं सुकेशी ।
शैब्या नीव्यां विधत्ते करमिति युगपन्माधवः प्रेयसीभिर्
भावेनाहूयमानो बहुशिखरमनाः पश्य कुण्ठो ऽयमास्ते ॥३६॥

yathā vā

padmā dṛgbhaṅgiralaṃ kalayati kamalā jṛmbhate sāṅgabhaṅgaṃ
tārā dormūlamalpaṃ prathayati kurute karṇakaṇḍūṃ sukeśī |
śaibyā nīvyāṃ vidhatte karamiti yugapanmādhavaḥ preyasībhir
bhāvenāhūyamāno bahuśikharamanāḥ paśya kuṇṭho 'yamāste ||36||

Or:

[*Vṛndā says this to Kundalatā.* (Viṣṇudāsa Gosvāmin, [VG])[29]]

Padmā sends signals with her eyes;
Kamalā yawns and stretches her body;
Tārā exposes her arm-pits slightly;
Sukeśī scratches at her ear;
Śaibyā places her hand on her hip.

Simultaneously Mādhava is beckoned
With deep passion, by many lovers.
Notice how he hesitates,
His mind flowing toward many points.[30] (14)

---

[29]Hereafter, Viṣṇudāsa Gosvāmin will be abbreviated as (VG).

[30]Un., 1.36. This is an example of Kṛṣṇa as the courteous paramour. Since neither Jīva or Viśvanātha mention the speaker of this verse, I have consulted the commentary of Viṣṇudāsa Gosvāmin. Viṣṇudāsa was a disciple of Kṛṣṇadāsa Kavirāja (16th-17th cents), the great biographer of Śrī Caitanya. Haridāsa Dāsa Bābā published an edition of his commentary, the *Svātma-pramodinī* (*For My Own Gratification*), based on a copy found in the Govinda-granthāgāra (the Govinda Library) in Jaipur. See the bibliograpy for the details.

अथ शठः

स्वप्ने व्यलीकं वनमालिनोक्तं
पालीत्युपाकर्ण्य विवर्णवक्त्रा ।
श्यामा विनिःश्वस्य मधुत्रियामां
सहस्रयामामिव सा व्यनैषीत् ॥३८॥

atha śaṭhaḥ

svapne vyalīkaṃ vanamālinoktaṃ
pālītyupākarṇya vivarṇavaktrā |
śyāmā viniḥśvasya madhutriyāmāṃ
sahasrayāmāmiva sā vyanaiṣīt ||38||

As Deceitful Lover:

[*A girlfriend of Śyāmā tells this to Nāndīmukhī. (V)*]

Vanamālī[31] said something offensive in (his) sleep.
Hearing "Pālī," Śyāmā paled and sighed deeply;
She passed the spring night
as though it were a thousand nights long.[32] (15)

[31]"Vanamālī" literally means "Wearer of a Garland of Forest Flowers," another name for Kṛṣṇa

[32]Un., 1.38. Kṛṣṇa has uttered the name of a rival of Śyāmā's, Pālī, in his sleep. He had assured Śyāmā that apart from her, no other woman appeals to him even in dream.

अथ धृष्टः

नखाङ्का न श्यामे घनघुसृणरेखाततिरियं
न लाक्षान्तःक्रुरे परिचिनु गिरेर्गैरिकमिदम् ।
धियं धत्से चित्रं वत मृगमदे ऽप्यञ्जनतया
तरुण्यास्ते दृष्टिः किमिव विपरीतस्थितिरभूत् ॥४१॥

atha dhṛṣṭaḥ

nakhāṅkā na śyāme ghanaghusṛṇarekhātatiriyaṃ
na lākṣāntaḥkrure paricinu girergairikamidam |
dhiyaṃ dhatse citraṃ vata mṛgamade 'pyañjanatayā
taruṇyāste dṛṣṭiḥ kimiva viparītasthitirabhūt ||41||

As Shameless Lover:

[*Kṛṣṇa lies to a devastated Śyāmā about the signs of another woman on his body. (V)*]

Śyāmā! These are not nailmarks!
These are (only) lines of thick saffron.
O cruel-hearted! This is not alta (lac)!
Can't you recognize this red chalk from the mountains?
It is amazing that you take musk to be collyrium.
How has the vision of a young girl like you
become so confused?[33] (16)

Thus ends the chapter on the Hero (Kṛṣṇa).

[33]Un., 1.41. This is Kṛṣṇa as deceitful paramour.

Kṛṣṇa and his Friends

Chapter Two: Companions of the Hero

अथैतस्य सहायाः स्युः पञ्चधा चेटको विटः ।
विदूषकः पीठमर्दः प्रियनर्मसखस्तथा ॥ १ ॥

athaitasya sahāyāḥ syuḥ pañcadhā ceṭako viṭaḥ |
vidūṣakaḥ pīṭhamardaḥ priyanarmasakhastathā ||1||

Now, [the hero's] five companions are:[1]
trusted servant (*ceṭaka*), parasite (*viṭa*),
jester (*vidūṣaka*), accomplice (*pīṭhamarda*)[2]
and fifth his dear playmate (*priya-narma-sakha*).[3] (1)

---

[1]Rūpa adds a companion, the *priya-narma-sakha* or dear play- or joke-mate, to Siṃhabhūpāla's traditional four (1.89cd, 90ab):

> *atha śṛṅgāranetṝṇāṃ sāhāyyakaraṇocitāḥ* ||
> *nirūpyante pīṭhamardaviṭaceṭavidūṣakāḥ* |

"Now, are described the seat-polisher, parasite, trusted servant, and buffoon who are fit to be friends of an erotic hero." [The trusted servant is not found in dramaturgical texts earlier than Siṃhabhūpāla (i.e., in Dhanañjaya or Śāradātanaya).]

[2]The *pīṭhamarda* (lit. polished-seat) is a bachelor friend of the hero who, if he were not so poor, would be a hero himself. He has many of the same qualities as the hero, only fewer and to a lesser degree. He gets his name because he carries everything he owns on his back—a red cloth, some soap for massages, and a special kind of polished seat with a single stick leg on which he sits. He often acts as a tutor for the hero in the arts of pleasure (*kāma*). See A.K Warder, *Indian Kāvya Literature*, vol. 1, para. 32, p. 14.

[3]Un., 2.1. This chapter's twenty-three poems show each of the five types of friends in action. Viśvanātha comments, following Jīva, that these friends are youths created by the power of sport (*līlā-śakti*) but, with the exception of the *pīṭhamarda*, they are like eunuchs, having no masculine feelings or desires. That is, they are not themselves amorously attracted to the village girls. Jīva, however, does not exclude the *pīṭhamarda* from this condition.

नर्मप्रयोगे नैपुण्यं सदा गाढानुरागिता।
देशकालज्ञता दाक्ष्यं रुष्टगोपीप्रसादनम् ।
निगूढमन्त्रतेत्याद्याः सहायानां गुणाः स्मृताः ॥२॥

narmaprayoge naipuṇyaṃ sadā gāḍhānurāgitā|
deśakālajñatā dākṣyaṃ ruṣṭagopīprasādanam |
nigūḍhamantratetyādyāḥ sahāyānāṃ guṇāḥ smṛtāḥ ||2||

The strengths of companions are:
expertise in telling jokes,
deep, undying attachment,
awareness of right time and place,
skillfulness in many things,
ability to pacify angry girls and
to provide private advice.[4] (2)

---

[4]Un., 2.2. Siṃhabhūpāla's list of the traits of the companions or helpers are listed in his Ras. (1.93-94ab):

> *deśakālajñatā bhāṣāmādhuryaṃ ca vidagdhatā |*
> *protsāhane kuśalatā yathoktakathanaṃ tathā ||*
> *nigūḍhamantratetyādyāḥ sahāyānāṃ guṇā matāḥ |*

Knowledge of place and time, sweetness of speech, cleverness, expertise in giving encouragement, telling something as it was told, giving confidential advice; these are the traits of the helpers.

न पुनरिदमपूर्वं देवि कुत्रापि दृष्टं
शरदि यदियमारान्माधवी पुष्पिताभूत् ।
इति किल वृषभानोर्लम्भितासौ कुमारी
व्रजनवयुवराज व्याजतः कुञ्जवीथिम् ॥४॥

na punaridamapūrvaṃ devi kutrāpi dṛṣṭaṃ
śaradi yadiyamārānmādhavī puṣpitābhūt |
iti kila vṛṣabhānorlambhitāsau kumārī
vrajanavayuvarāja vyājataḥ kuñjavīthim ||4||

A trusted servant-friend (ceṭa) tells Kṛṣṇa how he lured Rādhā toward him.

"Goddess! Such an unprecedented thing
has never before been seen 'round here—
That in the autumn,
a *mādhavī* vine[5]
has suddenly sprung blossoms."
Saying this, young prince of Vraja,
I put Vṛṣabhānu's daughter, Rādhā,
on the bower path towards you.[6] (3)

---

[5]Mādhavī vine clings to the mango tree as a symbol of an erotic young woman clinging to her lover. It blooms year-round, but is specially fragrant in early Spring.

[6]Un., 2.4. This is an example of a *ceṭa*'s ability to bring lovers together (*saṃdhāna-catura*).

व्रजे सारङ्गाक्षीविततिभिरनुल्लङ्घ्यवचनः
सखाहं तद्बन्धोश्चटुभिरभियाचे मुहुरिदम् ।
कलक्रीडद्वंशीस्थगितजगतीयौवतधृतिस्
त्वया युक्तः श्यामे न खलु परिहर्तुं सखि हरिः ॥६॥

vraje sāraṅgākṣīvitatibhiranullaṅghyavacanaḥ
sakhāhaṃ tadbandhoścaṭubhirabhiyāce muhuridam |
kalakrīḍadvaṃśīsthagitajagatīyauvatadhṛtis
tvayā yuktaḥ śyāme na khalu parihartuṃ sakhi hariḥ ||6||

The Parasite [or hanger-on] (*viṭa*):[7]

[*The smoothly sophisticated parasite (viṭa) talks Śyāmā into forgiving Kṛṣṇa.*]

The friend of your friend am I,
Whose words Vraja's doe-eyed girls cannot ignore.
With sweet words I plead once more:
Śyāmā! To give up Hari is not right,
the soft tones of whose flute
dissolve the resolves of young girls everywhere.[8] (4)

---

[7]Rūpa's characterization of the parasite is as follows:

> The parasite has mastery
> in fashionable dress and accessory;
> he's quite cunning and in gatherings rises above [others];
> he's well-versed, too, in the arts of love.

Rūpa again uses Siṃhabhūpāla's words from his Ras. (1.91cd): *kāmatantrakalāvedī viṭa ityabhidhīyate.* Warder has an interesting characterization of the "parasite" in para. 30 of his *Indian Kāvya Literature*, vol.1, pp. 13-14: "If the would-be *nāgaraka* [that is, hero] were not wealthy, three [other] careers in the service of *nāgarakas* and geishas were open to him, according to the *Kāma-sūtra*. If married, he could be a parasite [hanger-on], who is primarily a messenger and ambassador with wide experience of human nature, or he could become a 'jester' or 'fool' (*vidūṣaka*). The parasite [hanger-on] is expert in polite and quick-witted conversations and flattery and so lubricates social intercourse. It is his business to know everything that is going on in society. Though something of a rogue, he is on the whole a stickler for what he interprets as the proper social conventions and does not tolerate odd behavior or what seems to him immoral, i.e., departures from the usual custom. ... "

[8]Un., 2.4.

तुष्टेन स्मितपुष्पवृष्टिरधुना सद्यस्त्वया मुच्यताम्
आरूढः कुतुकी विमानमतुलं मां गोकुलाखण्डलः ।
इत्थं देवि मनोरथेन रभसादभ्यर्थ्यमानो ऽप्यसौ
यत्ते मानिनि नाधरः प्रयतते तन्नाद्भुतं रागिषु ॥८॥

tuṣṭena smitapuṣpavṛṣṭiradhunā sadyastvayā mucyatām
ārūḍhaḥ kutukī vimānamatulaṃ māṃ gokulākhaṇḍalaḥ |
itthaṃ devi manorathena rabhasādabhyarthyamāno 'pyasau
yatte mānini nādharaḥ prayatate tannādbhutaṃ rāgiṣu ||8||

Now the jester:[9]

[*The jester Madhumaṅgala helps Kṛṣṇa soften a lady's anger.*]

Be pleased now to quickly release
a shower of flower-smiles,
since the delightful lord of Gokula
has climbed aboard me,
an unmatched vehicle.

Even though your own mind-chariot,
Desire, begs you for smiles,
sulking lady, your lips do not respond:
not surprizing for such reddened [angered] objects.[10] (5)

[9]Abhinavagupta characterizes the jester or *vidūṣaka* as one who, in matters of sexual love, spoils (*dūṣayati*) agreement with discord or discord with agreement. When love-separation is present, he with pleasant discussions causes the hero to forget his woes.

[10]Un., 2.8.

यथा

कालिन्दीपुलिने मुकुन्दचरितं विश्वस्य विस्मापनं
द्रष्टुं गच्छति गोष्ठमेव निखिलं नैकात्र चन्द्रावली ।
ब्रूमस्तस्य सुहृत्तमाः स्वयममी पथ्यञ्च तथ्यञ्च ते
मा गोवर्धनमल्ल घट्टय मुधा गोवर्धनोद्धारिणम् ॥११॥

yathā

kālindīpuline mukundacaritaṃ viśvasya vismāpanaṃ
draṣṭuṃ gacchati goṣṭhameva nikhilaṃ naikātra candrāvalī |
brūmastasya suhṛttamāḥ svayamamī pathyañca tathyañca te
mā govardhanamalla ghaṭṭaya mudhā govardhanoddhāriṇam ||11||

Now the accomplice (*pīṭhamarda*):

[*Accomplice Śrīdāman soothes Candrāvalī's jealous husband* (J)]

The acts of Mukunda[11]
on the bank of the Kālindī,
astounding to the whole world,
the entire village goes to see—
not just Candrāvalī.
We, his best of friends, advise
what is wholesome and wise for you;
Govardhana,[12] *Wrestler*, don't stir him up needlessly,
he who lifted *Mount* Govardhana up to the skies.[13] (6)

---

[11]"Giver of Liberation," Kṛṣṇa.

[12]Govardhana means "cow-nourisher" or "sense-enhancer" [wiki]. It's the name of the mountain near Vṛndāvana which Kṛṣṇa famously lifted and used as an umbrella to shade his companions.

[13]Un., 2.11. See "Tṛtīyakaḥ phenakaḥ" by Sreeramula Rajeswara Sarma in *Journal of European Ayurvedic Society* 2 (1992): 115-123 for argument that *pīṭhamarda* is a sophisticated, but impoverished person who gives massages and advice to the hero.

यथा

प्रत्यावर्तयति प्रसाद्य ललनां क्रीडाकलिप्रस्थितां
शय्यां कुञ्जगृहे करोत्यघभिदः कन्दर्पलीलोचिताम् ।
स्विन्नं बीजयति प्रियाहृदि परिस्त्रस्ताङ्गमुच्चैरमुं
क्व श्रीमानधिकारितां न सुबलः सेवाविधौ विन्दति ॥१४॥

yathā

pratyāvartayati prasādya lalanāṃ krīḍākaliprasthitāṃ
śayyāṃ kuñjagrhe karotyaghabhidaḥ kandarpalīlocitām |
svinnaṃ bījayati priyāhṛdi parisrastāṅgamuccairamuṃ
kva śrīmānadhikāritāṃ na subalaḥ sevāvidhau vindati ||14||

The dear playmate (*priya-narma-sakha*):

[*This statement of Rūpamañjarī to her friend is meant to produce new respect for Kṛṣṇa's friend Subala.* (V)]

To the performance of what service
has fortunate Subala not gained the right?
He pacifies and brings back a woman, who has
run away because of a quarrel during love-play.
In the bower house, he makes the bed of Agha's killer[14]
fit for games of love, and vigorously fans
Kṛṣṇa's perspiring body when it has fallen,
exhausted, onto the breast of his lover.[15] (7)

Thus ends the chapter on the Companions of the Hero.

[14]Kṛṣṇa as a child walked into the mouth off the demon Agha, who had taken the form of a giant python and swallowed his friends. Then he enlarged himself until the python's head burst.

[15]Un., 2.14

Beloved Ladies of Hari

Chapter Three: The Beloved Ladies of Hari

यथा

सुनिर्माणे धर्माध्वनि पतिपराभिः परिचिते
मुदा बद्धश्रद्धा गिरि च गुरुवर्गस्य परितः ।
गृहे याः सेवन्ते प्रियमपरतन्त्राः प्रतिदिनं
महिष्यस्ताः शौरेस्तव मुदमुदग्रां विदधतु ॥५॥

yathā

sunirmāṇe dharmādhvani patiparābhiḥ paricite
mudā baddhaśraddhā giri ca guruvargasya paritaḥ |
gṛhe yāḥ sevante priyamaparatantrāḥ pratidinaṃ
mahiṣyastāḥ śaurestava mudamudagrāṃ vidadhatu ||5||

The beloved ladies of Hari:[1]

[The beloved ladies of Hari are of two types: *svakīyā* (belonging to or married to Kṛṣṇa) and *parakīyā* (belonging to or married to someone else).]

The wives (*svakīyā*):

[*Draupadī says this to a friend.* (V)]

His queens' faith is joyfully fixed
on the well-made path of *dharma*,
well-known to wives devoted to their husbands.
Their faith is also fixed entirely in the words of their elders;
At home they serve their dear husband independently every day.
May they, Śauri's queens, give you great pleasure![2] (1)

---

[1]Rūpa describes the beloved ladies of Hari (*harivallabha*) as follows (Un., 3.1):

The beloved ladies of Hari
possess all the common good qualities,
but are the foremost bearers
of great love and sweetness.

These "common" or general good qualities are glossed by Viśvanātha as having pleasing bodies, all the good character traits, and so forth.

[2]Un., 3.5. Śauri, Kṛṣṇa, "the descendent of Śūra (Kṛṣṇa's grandfather)."

यथा

आर्या चेदतिवत्सला मयि मुहुर्गोष्ठेश्वरी किं ततः
प्राणेभ्यः प्रणयास्पदं प्रियसखीवृन्दं किमेतेन मे ।
वैकुण्ठाटवीमण्डलीविजयी चेद्वृन्दावनं तेन किं
दीव्यत्यत्र न चेदुमाव्रतफलं पिच्छावतंसी पतिः ॥३.१५॥

yathā

āryā cedativatsalā mayi muhurgoṣṭheśvarī kiṃ tataḥ
prāṇebhyaḥ praṇayāspadaṃ priyasakhīvṛndaṃ kimetena me |
vaikuṇṭhāṭavīmaṇḍalīvijayī cedvṛndāvanaṃ tena kiṃ
dīvyatyatra na cedumāvrataphalaṃ picchāvataṃsī patiḥ ||3.15||

Another example:

[*One of the maidens of Vṛndāvana who prayed to Goddess Kātyāyanī for Kṛṣṇa to become her husband says:*[3]]

If the venerable queen of the village
is often affectionate to me, what of it?
And what does it matter to me
that my beloved friends
Are dearer than my own life?
So what if Vṛndāvana
outshines the orbs of Vaikuṇṭha,[4]
if my vow to Umā[5] does not result in
my husband who wears a peacock's feather
playing here?[6] (2)

---

[3]See verse 9 of Chapter One.

[4]Viṣṇu's heaven.

[5]Śiva's wife Pārvatī. Also known as Kātyāyanī.

[6]Un., 3.15. Though they are not actually married to Kṛṣṇa, because they thought of him as their husband, some of the girls of Vṛndāvana are considered to belong together with his wives. Rūpa says just before this verse (Un. 3.14):

Among the maidens of Gokula
who think Hari is their husband,
their being possessed by Kṛṣṇa
is not at all improper,
because they firmly believe
that he is indeed that for them.

यथा

रागोल्लासविलङ्घितार्यपदवीविश्रान्तयो ऽप्युद्धुर-
श्रद्धारज्यदरुन्धतीमुखसतीवृन्देन वन्द्येहिताः ।
आरण्या अपि माधुरीपरिमलव्याक्षिप्तलक्ष्मीश्रियस्
तास्त्रैलोक्यविलक्षणा ददतु वः कृष्णस्य सख्यः सुखम् ॥१८॥

yathā

rāgollāsavilaṅghitāryapadavīviśrāntayo 'pyuddhura-
śraddhārajyadarundhatīmukhasatīvṛndena vandyehitāḥ |
āraṇyā api mādhurīparimalavyākṣiptalakṣmīśriyas
tāstrailokyavilakṣaṇā dadatu vaḥ kṛṣṇasya sakhyaḥ sukham ||18||

His inamorata (*parakīyā*):[7]

[*Paurṇamāsī addresses this to Nāndīmukhī, Gārgī, and others who were just beginning to act as messenger/go-betweens for Kṛṣṇa and his lovers:* (V)]

Although they have stepped outside of the serene
path of the respected because of their rising passion,
their actions still are praised by chaste women
like Arundhatī, radiant with faith.
And although they are mere forest dwellers,
the fragrance of their sweet natures
casts down even the beauty of Lakṣmī.

May they, the sweethearts of Kṛṣṇa,
who are unlike any others in the three worlds,
bless you all with happiness.[8] (3)

---

[7]Rūpa defines this type of lover as follows (Un. 3.17):

They offer themselves out of love alone,
caring nothing for the two worlds (this world and the next);
nor are they accepted in marriage;
they are the women of others.

Parakīyās are of two types: those who are unwed and those who are married to others. Moreover, Rūpa says (Un.,3.19):

They are mostly famous as the women
Who dwell in the pasturelands
Of the Lord of Vraja (Nanda).
The concealment of their desire there
Gives pleasure to the Prince of Gokula (Kṛṣṇa).

[8]Un., 3.18.

यथा तत्रैव (१०.३२.२२)

न पारये ऽहं निरवद्यसंयुजां
स्वसाधुकृत्यं विबुधायुषापि वः ।
या माभजन्दुर्जरगेहशृङ्खलाः
संवृश्च्य तद्वः प्रतियातु साधुना ॥२९॥

yathā tatraiva (10.32.22)

na pāraye 'haṃ niravadyasaṃyujāṃ
svasādhukṛtyaṃ vibudhāyuṣāpi vaḥ |
yā mābhajandurjaragehaśṛṅkhalāḥ
saṃvṛścya tadvaḥ pratiyātu sādhunā ||29||

Hari himself speaks of the superiority of the paramour:

[*Kṛṣṇa speaks*]

Even with a lifetime of a god,
I am unable to repay the good deeds
of you whose connection (with me) is faultless.
You've cut the strong chains of the home
and come to me.
Let your own goodness be your repayment.[9] (4)

[9]Bhāg., 10.32.22 cited in Un. at 3.29.

यथा (भाग. १०.४७.६१)

आसामहो चरणरेणुजुषामहं स्यां
वृन्दावने किमपि गुल्मलतौषधीनाम् ।
या दुस्त्यजं स्वजनमार्यपथं च हित्वा
भेजुर्मुकुन्दपदवीं श्रुतिभिर्विमृग्याम् ॥३१॥

yathā (bhāg. 10.47.61)

āsāmaho caraṇareṇujuṣāmahaṃ syāṃ
vṛndāvane kimapi gulmalatauṣadhīnām |
yā dustyajaṃ svajanamāryapathaṃ ca hitvā
bhejurmukundapadavīṃ śrutibhirvimṛgyām ||31||

Uddhava, Kṛṣṇa's best friend in Mathurā, proclaims the superiority of the paramour as well.

[*Uddhava says in the* Bhāgavata Purāṇa:]

Alas, let me become one of the
bushes, vines, or herbs in Vṛndāvana,

which gather the dust from the feet of these women[10]
who gave up family and the path of the respected
(a road which is hard to leave)
and went the path of Mukunda[11]
which is sought for even by the Vedas.[12] (5)

---

[10]*gopīs*

[11]A name of Kṛṣṇa which by dubious etymology is said to mean: "giver of liberation." See the *Bhāgavata Purāṇa*, 1.9.38, for instance.

[12]Bhāg., 10.47.61 cited at Un., 3.31. Viśvanātha poses a question to Uddhava: "you are one of Kṛṣṇa's foremost companions in his sport. What do you see as different about the women of Vraja?" The answer is implied by the word *dustyajam*, "hard to give up." The path of respect, that is, the conventional moral code imposed by one's society and one's family, is hard to give up. The love of the women of Vraja for Kṛṣṇa is unconditional (*nirupādhi*). Such love is not found in the love of Kṛṣṇa's queens in Dvārakā which is conditioned by conventional moral codes.

यथा

विस्रब्धा सखि धूलिकेलिषु पटासंवीतवक्षःस्थला
बालासीति न वल्लवस्तव पिता जामातरं मृग्यति ।
त्वन्तु भ्रान्तविलोचनान्तमचिरादाकर्ण्य वृन्दावने
कूजन्तीं शिखिपिच्छमौलिमुरलीं सोत्कम्पमाघूर्णसि ॥३६॥

yathā

visrabdhā sakhi dhūlikeliṣu paṭāsaṃvītavakṣaḥsthalā
bālāsīti na vallavastava pitā jāmātaraṃ mṛgyati |
tvantu bhrāntavilocanāntamacirādākarṇya vṛndāvane
kūjantīṃ śikhipicchamaulimuralīṃ sotkampamāghūrṇasi ||36||

Among the paramours the unmarried maiden (*kanyakā*):[13]

[*This is jokingly spoken to a maiden by the wife of her older brother, who has herself been with Kṛṣṇa:* (J, V)]

O Friend, you, confident in your powder games—
your cloth has fallen from your breasts.

Since you are a child,
your cowherd father is not yet searching for a husband.

But you, suddenly hearing the call of the flute
of him whose head is decked with peacock feathers
in Vṛdāvana—
with your glance flashing about,
you are spinning around, shivering.[14] (6)

---

[13]Rūpa describes the unmarried maidens (*kanyakā*) as follows (Un., 3.34):

The maidens are unwed, bashful,
under the protection of their fathers,
confident in games with their friends,
and mostly marked by innocence.

[14]Un., 3.36.

यथा पद्यावल्याम् (३११)

कात्यायनीकुसुमकामनया किमर्थं
कान्तारकुक्षिकुहरं कुतुकाद्गतासि ।
सद्यस्तनं स्तनयुगे तव कण्टकाङ्कं
पत्युः स्वसा सखि सशङ्कमुदीक्षते ऽसौ ॥३८॥

yathā padyāvalyām (311)

kātyāyanīkusumakāmanayā kimartham
kāntārakukṣikuharaṃ kutukādgatāsi |
sadyastanaṃ stanayuge tava kaṇṭakāṅkaṃ
patyuḥ svasā sakhi saśaṅkamudīkṣate 'sau ||38||

The woman married to another.[15]

[*Padmā says this to Candrāvalī:* (V)]

Why did you go so eagerly
into that cave in the middle
of the wilderness looking for flowers
to offer to Kātyāyanī?
Your husband's sister looks suspiciously,
friend, at those fresh "thorn scratches" on your breasts.[16]
(7)

---

[15]Rūpa characterizes the paramour married to another in the following way (Un., 3.37):

These are more excellent than all
in the grandeur of their beauty
and virtue; greater than even Ramā's
is their selfless love and sweetness.

Ramā is another name for Lakṣmī or Śrī, the goddess of fortune.

[16]*Necklace of Verses* (*Padyāvalī*), 311 cited at Un., 3.38. This is given as Rūpa's own composition in the *Padyāvalī*. The second half of this verse as found in the *Padyāvalī* is different from the version here:

paśya stanastavakayos tava kaṇṭakāṅkaṃ
gopaḥ sukaṇṭhi bata paśyati jātakopaḥ||

Look, Sweet-voiced girl! Your husband
is looking at the thorn scratches
on your budlike breasts in anger.

तत्र शास्त्रसिद्धास्तु राधा चन्द्रावली तथा ।
विशाखा ललिता श्यामा पद्मा शैब्या च भद्रिका ।
तारा विचित्रा गोपाली धनिष्ठा पालिकादयः ॥५६॥

चन्द्रावल्येव सोमाभा गान्धर्वा राधिकैव सा ।
अनुराधा तु ललिता नैतास्तेनोदिताः पृथक् ॥५७॥

tatra śāstrasiddhāstu rādhā candrāvalī tathā |
viśākhā lalitā śyāmā padmā śaibyā ca bhadrikā |
tārā vicitrā gopālī dhaniṣṭhā pālikādayaḥ ||56||

candrāvalyeva somābhā gāndharvā rādhikaiva sā |
anurādhā tu lalitā naitāstenoditāḥ pṛthak ||57||

Those who are well-known in scripture
Are Rādhā and Candrāvalī,
Viśākhā, Lalitā, Śyāmā,
Padmā, Śaibyā, Bhadrikā, and Tārā,
Vicitrā, Gopālī, and Dhaniṣṭhā,
Pālikā, and others as well. (8)

Candrāvalī is Somābhā
And Rādhikā is Gāndharvā;
Lalitā is Anurādhā;
Thus, these are not named separately.[17] (9)

Thus ends Chapter Three on the Beloved Ladies of the Hari.

[17]Un., 3.56-57. By scripture is meant the *Bhaviṣyottara Purāṇa*, the *Prahlāda-saṃhitā* of the *Skandha Purāṇa*, and other less well known texts. Both Śrī Jīva and Viśvanātha quote a verse from the first of these:

gopālī pālikā dhanyā
viśākhā dhyānaniṣṭhikā |
rādhānurādhā somābhā
tārakā daśamī tathā ||
Gopālī, Pālikā, Dhanyā
Viśākhā, Dhyānaniṣṭhikā
Rādhā, Anurādhā, and Somābhā,
Tārakā, also Daśamī.

Daśamī either refers to Tārakā as the "tenth" woman or is the name of another woman who is the tenth. In this verse, according to Jīva and Viśvanātha, Anurādhā is Lalitā and Somābhā is Candrāvalī. The second text adds: Lalitā, Padmā, Bhadrā, Śaibyā, and Śyāmalā. The *Gopāla-tāpanī Upaniṣad* refers to Rādhā as Gāndharvā. Among these Rādhā and Candrāvalī are here separated out as the best.

Rādhā Lamenting with her Confidante

Chapter Four: Śrī Rādhā

तत्रापि सर्वथा श्रेष्ठे राधाचन्द्रावलीत्युभे ।
यूथयोस्तु ययोः सन्ति कोटिसङ्ख्या मृगीदृशः ॥ १ ॥

tatrāpi sarvathā śreṣṭhe rādhācandrāvalītyubhe |
yūthayostu yayoḥ santi koṭisaṅkhyā mṛgīdṛśaḥ ||1||

Here the two best in every way
are Rādhā and Candrāvalī,
in whose two followings are found
millions of doe-eyed ladies.[1] (1)

[1]Un., 4.1. Among all the beloved ladies of Kṛṣṇa mentioned in the last chapter, two stand out as having particularly deep and powerful love for Kṛṣna: Rādhā and Candrāvalī.

तयोरप्युभयोर्मध्ये राधिका सर्वथाधिका ।
महाभावस्वरूपेयं गुणैरतिवरीयसी ॥३॥

tayorapyubhayormadhye rādhikā sarvathādhikā |
mahābhāvasvarūpeyaṃ guṇairativarīyasī ||3||

But between the two, Rādhikā
Is in every way superior;
She's the essence of Great Love[2]
And in merits more excellent.[3] (2)

[2]*Mahābhāva*: the greatest or highest state of love. It is defined and exemplified in the fourteenth chapter of the *Blazing Sapphire* (14.156). Rūpa characterizes it thus:

mukundamahiṣīvṛndairapyasāvatidurlabhaḥ |
vrajadevyekasaṃvedyo mahābhāvākhyayocyate ||

Even for Mukunda's queens
it is extremely hard to achieve.
It is only experienced
by the ladies of Vraja;
as "*mahābhāva*" is it known.

Mahābhāva can be translated "the grand emotion." *Bhāva* also means "state" or "condition." The problem here is that this verse does not really distinguish Rādhā from Candrāvalī. Both are ladies of Vraja. Within the condition of *mahābhāva*, however, there are several refinements (e.g. developed [*rūḍha*] and highly developed [*adhirūḍha*]), and subdivisions called delight ([*modana*] and exhilaration [*mādana*]), which distinguish Rādhā and her group from Candrāvalī and her group.

[3]Un., 1.3.

ह्लादिनी या महाशक्तिः सर्वशक्तिवरीयसी ।
तत्सारभावरूपेयमिति तन्त्रे प्रतिष्ठिता ॥६॥

hlādinī yā mahāśaktiḥ sarvaśaktivarīyasī |
tatsārabhāvarūpeyamiti tantre pratiṣṭhitā ||6||

That great power which gives pleasure,
Of all the powers best beyond measure,
its core condition—of that is she formed.[45] (3)

---

[4]The pleasure-giving power is called the *hlādinī-śakti*. It is one of three divine powers believed to belong to and to be inseparable from the Lord. Jīva cites the major proof texts for those three powers. The best known comes from the *Viṣṇu Purāṇa* (1.12.69):

> *hlādinī saṃdhinī saṃvit tvayy ekā sarvasaṃsthitau* |
> *hlādatāpakarī miśrā tvayi no guṇavarjite* ||
>
> The pleasure-giving, connecting,
> knowledge-producing powers are
> one in you who are perpetual.
> [Separate strands] causing pleasure and heat
> and mixing exist not in you,
> who are free from guṇa-threads.

He next cites a less well known work called the *Sarvajña-sūkta* (*Wise Sayings of the All-knowing One*). This may be from the lost commentary on the *Vedānta-sūtra* attributed to Viṣṇusvāmin. Fragments of the commentary are quoted in the commentary of Śrīdhara on the *Viṣṇu Purāṇa* (1.7.6):

> *hlādinyā saṃvidā śliṣṭaḥ saccidānanda īśvaraḥ* |
> *avidyāsaṃvṛtto jīvaḥ saṃkleśanikarākaraḥ* ||
>
> Embraced by the pleasure-giving
> and knowledge-making powers
> is the Controller who is
> being, knowledge, and bliss.
> The living being is covered
> by ignorance, a figure of afflictions.

The "core condition" (*sāra-bhāva*) of that great pleasure-giving power means, according to Jīva, the state known as *mādana* (exhilaration), the highest expression of *mahābhāva*, the great emotion. Rādhā has become identified with that state. (J) See Chapter 14, verse 219 and following.

So in Tantra is it confirmed.

[5]Un., 4.6. The tantra referred to here is the *Bṛhad-gautamīya Tantra*.

तत्र सुष्ठुकान्तस्वरूपा, यथा

कचास्तव सुकुञ्चिता मुखमधीरदीर्घेक्षणं
कठोरकुचभागुरः क्रशिमशालि मध्यस्थलम् ।
नते शिरसि दोर्लते करजरत्नरम्यौ करौ
विधूनयति राधिके त्रिजगदेष रूपोत्सवः ॥८॥

tatra suṣṭhukāntasvarūpā, yathā

kacāstava sukuñcitā mukhamadhīradīrghekṣaṇaṃ
kaṭhorakucabhāguraḥ kraśimaśāli madhyasthalam |
nate śirasi dorlate karajaratnaramyau karau
vidhūnayati rādhike trijagadeṣa rūpotsavaḥ ||8||

Rādhā's Surpassing Beauty:

[*This is spoken to Rādhā by Kṛṣṇa.* (J) (V)]

Your hair has lovely curls,
your face large roving eyes;
Full breasts fill up your chest;
your waist is thin in size;
your shoulders slope gently;
your jewel-nailed hands delight.
Your festival of beauty, Rādhikā,
shakes the three worlds left and right.[6] (4)

---

[6]Un., 4.8. Rādhā's attractive nature is indicated in the previous didactic verse (4.7):

suṣṭhukāntasvarūpeyaṃ sarvadā vārṣabhānavī |
dhṛtaṣoḍaśaśṛṅgārā dvādaśābharaṇānvitā ||7||

This Vārṣabhānavī [Rādhā, the daughter of Vṛṣabhānu] does ever possess
A nature of surpassing attractiveness,
Sixteen amorous modes of grooming
And twelve erotic ornamentations.

Her sixteen amorous modes of grooming are listed in the next verse (Un., 4.9) in this collection. The verse presenting the twelve erotic ornaments (Un., 4.10) has not been included here. They are: a flower in her hair, gold earings, gold belt, gold brooch, pairs of hoops and bars in her ears, throat ornaments, finger rings, necklaces with star-like pearls, arm bands, ankle bells set with jewels, and toe-rings.

अथ धृतषोडशशृङ्गारा

स्नाता नासाग्रजाग्रन्मणिरसितपटा सूत्रिणी बद्धवेणी
सोत्तंसा चर्चिताङ्गी कुसुमितचिकुरा स्रग्विणी पद्महस्ता ।
ताम्बूलास्योरुबिन्दुस्तवकितचिबुका कज्जलाक्षी सुचित्रा
राधालक्तोज्ज्वलाङ्घ्रिः स्फुरिति तिलकिनी षोडशाकल्पिनीयम् ॥९॥

atha dhṛtaṣoḍaśaśṛṅgārā

snātā nāsāgrajāgranmaṇirasitapaṭā sūtriṇī baddhaveṇī
sottaṃsā carcitāṅgī kusumitacikurā sragviṇī padmahastā |
tāmbūlāsyorubindustavakitacibukā kajjalākṣī sucitrā
rādhālaktojjvalāṅghriḥ sphuriti tilakinī ṣoḍaśākalpinīyam ||9||

Her sixteen preparations for love:

[*Subala says this to Kṛṣṇa while they are on their way to the pasture and notice Rādhā in a nearby garden:* (V)]

Freshly bathed, her nose-jewel sparkling,
waist string tightened on her deep blue skirt—
her hair's been braided, body massaged
with paste someone made from sandalwood.
Strands of flowers deck her ears
and more flowers are woven into her curls.
Garlands curve around her neck
and between her fingers a lotus twirls.
Wood-scented betel-nut freshens her breath.
Flowers on her chin have been drawn with musk.
And kājal-smoke shadows her eyes.
Above, on her brow, a sacred sign glows—
three vertical lines and a dot mark the space.
Flowers drawn with muskpaste bloom on her cheeks
and her feet have been reddened with lac.
Rādhā, picture of perfect beauty, entices
with sixteen amorous embellishments.[7] (5)

[7]Un., 4.9.

अथ वृन्दावनेश्वर्याः कीर्त्यन्ते प्रवरा गुणाः ।
मधुरेयं नववयाश्चलापाङ्गोज्ज्वलस्मिता ॥ ११ ॥

चारुसौभाग्यरेखाढ्या गन्धोन्मादितमाधवा ।
सङ्गीतप्रसराभिज्ञा रम्यवाङ्नर्मपण्डिता ॥ १२ ॥

विनीता करुणापूर्णा विदग्धा पाटवान्विता ।
लज्जाशीला सुमर्यादा धैर्यगाम्भीर्यशालिनी ॥ १३ ॥

सुविलासा महाभावपरमोत्कर्षतर्षिणी ।
गोकुलप्रेमवसतिर्जगच्छ्रेणीलसद्यशाः ॥ १४ ॥

atha vṛndāvaneśvaryāḥ kīrtyante pravarā guṇāḥ |
madhureyaṃ navavayāścalāpāṅgojjvalasmitā ||11||

cārusaubhāgyarekhāḍhyā gandhonmāditamādhavā |
saṅgītaprasarābhijñā ramyavāṅnarmapaṇḍitā ||12||

vinītā karuṇāpūrṇā vidagdhā pāṭavānvitā |
lajjāśīlā sumaryādā dhairyagāmbhīryaśālinī ||13||

suvilāsā mahābhāvaparamotkarṣatarṣiṇī |
gokulapremavasatirjagacchreṇīlasadyaśāḥ ||14||

Now we praise the great personal qualities
of the Mistress of Vṛndāvana:[8]
she's sweet, she's young, her side-glance
is quick, her smile is brilliant. (6)

She has endearing lines of good fortune.
Her fragrance drives Mādhava mad.
She knows an enormous assortment of songs.
Her speech delights, in wit she's a whiz. (7)

She's humble, compassionate, and clever;
She's skillful, shy, and polite,
She's always composed and deeply profound. (8)

Yet she is playful, and thirsts for
the Great Emotion's[9] exalted shore;
The lodestar of Gokula's love,
her fame shines bright in many worlds.[10] (9)

---

[8]Śrī Rādhikā.
[9]*Mahābhāva*
[10]Un., 4.11-14.

अथ नववयाः

श्रोणिः स्यन्दनतां कृशोदरि कुचद्वन्द्वं क्रमाच्चक्रतां
भ्रूश्चापश्रियमीक्षणद्वयमिदं यात्याशुगत्वं तव ।
सैनापत्यमतः प्रदाय भुवि ते कामः पशूनां पतिं
धुन्वञ्जित्वरमानिनं त्वयि निजं साम्राज्यभारं न्यधात् ॥२१॥

atha navavayāḥ

śroṇiḥ syandanatāṃ kṛśodari kucadvandvaṃ kramāccakratāṃ
bhrūścāpaśriyamīkṣaṇadvayamidaṃ yātyāśugatvaṃ tava |
saināpatyamataḥ pradāya bhuvi te kāmaḥ paśūnāṃ patiṃ
dhunvañjitvaramāninaṃ tvayi nijaṃ sāmrājyabhāraṃ nyadhāt ||21||

Now her youth:
[*This is spoken by one of the female messengers.* (J) (V)]

Your buttocks have begun to roll,
Your breasts now round and full,
And gradually, thin-waisted girl,
Through eyebrows shaped like bows,
Your double glances have become quick-quick.
Yes, the Lord of Love gave you
the post of his commander on earth
And placed his kingdom in your care,
You who unsettle and defeat
the mighty lord of beasts.[11] (10)

---

[11]Un., 4.21.

अथ चलापाङ्गी

तडिदतिचलतां ते किं दृगन्तादपाठी-
द्विधुमुखि तडितो वा किं तवायं दृगन्तः ।
ध्रुवमिह गुरुताभूत्त्वद्दृगन्तस्य राधे
वरमतिजविनां मे येन जिग्ये मनो ऽपि ॥२२॥

atha calāpāṅgī

taḍidaticalatāṃ te kiṃ dṛgantādapāṭhī-
dvidhumukhi taḍito vā kiṃ tavāyaṃ dṛgantaḥ |
dhruvamiha gurutābhūttvaddṛgantasya rādhe
varamatijavināṃ me yena jigye mano 'pi ||22||

And her wandering glance:

[*Kṛṣṇa says this to Rādhā:* (J) (V)]

Has lightning taken lessons in
Quickness from your sidelong glance?
Or, Moonface, has this glance of yours
Learned its speed from lightning?
Surely here the role of teacher
Belonged to your glance, Rādhā,
Since even my mind it does beat—
Which is the best of things most fleet.[12] (11)

[12]Un., 4.22.

अथ गन्धोन्मादितमाधवा

वल्लीमण्डलपल्लवालिभिरितः सङ्गोपनायात्मनो
मा वृन्दावनचक्रवर्तिनि कृथा यत्नं मुधा माधवि ।
भ्राम्यद्भिः स्वविरोधिभिः परिमलैरुन्मादनैः सूचितां
कृष्णस्त्वां भ्रमाधिपः सखि धुवन्धूर्तो ध्रुवं धास्यति ॥२५॥

atha gandhonmāditamādhavā

vallīmaṇḍalapallavālibhiritaḥ saṅgopanāyātmano
mā vṛndāvanacakravartini kṛthā yatnaṃ mudhā mādhavi |
bhrāmyadbhiḥ svavirodhibhiḥ parimalairunmādanaiḥ sūcitāṃ
kṛṣṇastvāṃ bhramādhipaḥ sakhi dhuvandhūrto dhruvaṃ dhāsyati ||25||

Her fragrance that maddens Mādhava:

[*Her friend Tuṅgavidyā says this to Rādhā:* (V)]

To hide yourself surrounded here
By circles of vines, blossoms, and bees—
Do not spend your efforts in vain,
Honey-sweet Empress of Vṛndāvana.
Your intoxicating fragrance,
Wandering on the breeze, works against you,
Gives you away. Cunning Kṛṣṇa,
King of bees, trembling, will always find you.[13] (12)

[13]Un., 4.25.

यथा वा, विदग्धमाधवे (५.१५)

भूयो भूयः कलिविलसितैः सापराधापि राधा
श्लाघ्येनाहं यदघरिपुणा बाढमङ्गीकृतास्मि ।
तत्र क्षामोदरि किमपरं कारणं वः सखीनां
दत्तामोदां प्रगुणकरुणामञ्जरीमन्तरेण ॥ ३१ ॥

yathā vā, vidagdhamādhave (5.15)

bhūyo bhūyaḥ kalivilasitaiḥ sāparādhāpi rādhā
ślāghyenāhaṃ yadagharipuṇā bāḍhamaṅgīkṛtāsmi |
tatra kṣāmodari kimaparaṃ kāraṇaṃ vaḥ sakhīnām
dattāmodām praguṇakaruṇāmañjarīmantareṇa ||31||

Her humility:

For instance in *Clever Mādhava* (5.15):

[*Rādhā says to her friends:*]

> Though Rādhā again and again
> offends him with quarrelsome remarks,
> yet I am indeed accepted
> as praiseworthy by Sin's Enemy.[14]
>
> What reason could there be for that—
> other than the acts of compassion
> which happily blossom from you,
> my slender friends?[15] (13)

---

[14]Agharipu, the Enemy of Agha, i.e., Kṛṣṇa. Agha can mean "sin," but generally it refers to the demon Agha (Aghāsura) whom Kṛṣṇa kills in the form of a snake during his childhood in Vṛndāvana. See *Bhāgavata Purāṇa*. 10.12.13-39.

[15]Un., 4.31. There is a play here on Rādhā's name which is almost the same as the word *aparādha*, offense: *sāparādhā rādhā*, "offensive Rādhā." And, indeed, one set of meanings of the root $\sqrt{\textit{rādh}}$ is "to hurt, injure, destroy, exterminate." (V)

अथ विदग्धा

आचार्या धातुचित्रे पचनविरचनाचातुरीचारुचित्ता
वाग्युद्धे मुग्धयन्ती गुरुमपि च गिरां पण्डिता माल्यगुम्फे ।
पाठे शारीशुकानां पटुरजितमपि द्यूतकेलिषु जिष्णु-
र्विद्याविद्योतिबुद्धिः स्फुरति रतिकलाशालिनी राधिकेयम् ॥३३॥

atha vidagdhā

ācāryā dhātucitre pacanaviracanācāturīcārucittā
vāgyuddhe mugdhayantī gurumapi ca girāṃ paṇḍitā mālyagu-mphe |
pāṭhe śārīśukānāṃ paṭurajitamapi dyūtakeliṣu jiṣṇu-
rvidyāvidyotibuddhiḥ sphurati ratikalāśālinī rādhikeyam ||33||

Her cleverness:

[*Kundalatā says this to another pastoral woman who has asked: "What sort of talents has Rādhā, whose birth I witnessed not so long ago, developed?* (V)]

She's an *ācārya*[16] at painting pictures;
Her beautiful mind is expert
At inventing delightful new foods;
In word battles she can outwit
Even the teacher of language;
She is proficient at stringing garlands;
In reciting she has the craft
Of clever mynah birds and parrots;
At games of dice she can defeat
Even someone undefeated.

This Rādhikā—distinguished in
The arts and practices of love—
Her intellect—illuminating all
Fields of knowledge—is brilliant.[17] (14)

---

[16]A *guru* who teaches by example.
[17]Un., 4.33.

अथ लज्जाशीला

व्रजनरपतिसूनुर्दुर्लभालोकनो ऽयं
स्फुरति रहसि ताम्यत्येष तर्षाज्जनो ऽपि ।
विरम सखि लज्जे किञ्चिदुद्घाट्य वक्त्रं
निमिषमिह मनागप्यक्षिकोणं क्षिपामि ॥३५॥

atha lajjāśīlā

vrajanarapatisūnurdurlabhālokano 'yaṃ
sphurati rahasi tāmyatyeṣa tarṣājjano 'pi |
virama sakhi lajje kiñcidudghāṭya vaktraṃ
nimiṣamiha manāgapyakṣikoṇaṃ kṣipāmi ||35||

Her bashfulness:

[*Rādhā says this*:]

This son of the King of Vraja,
    who is so difficult to meet,
appears now where we are alone,
        but this thirsting person is frozen.

Friend Bashfulness! Unlock my face a little and stop
    just for a moment
        so that I can glance at him.[18] (15)

[18]Un., 4.35. Viśvanātha suggests that in calling bashfulness "friend," Rādhā really means the opposite, "enemy." "Will you take away my life?" Or, if we take it to really mean friend, Rādhā means to say: "Out of friendship I instruct you in what is best. Otherwise, if I die, where will you stay? Consider the consequences of that yourself. Then again I am only asking you to release one eye. You can rule the rest of my body. And release that one eye for just an instant and just a little. Your oppression will remain in place and I will continue to live. Just do this much."

अथ सुमर्यादा

प्राणानकृताहारा सखि राधाचातकी वरं त्यजति ।
न तु कृष्णमुदिरमुक्तादमृताद्वृत्तिं भजेदपराम् ॥३६॥

atha sumaryādā

prāṇānakṛtāhārā sakhi rādhācātakī varaṃ tyajati |
na tu kṛṣṇamudiramuktādamṛtādvṛttiṃ bhajedaparām ||36||

Her sense of propriety:

[*Spoken by Rādhā in response to one of her friends who urges her to eat. (J)*]

> Friend, this pied cuckoo,[19] Rādhā,
> would rather die of thirst, starve without eating,
> than live on any food except nectar
> released by that dark raincloud, Kṛṣṇa.[20] (16)

[19]*cātakī* = a female of the *cucculus melanoleucus* species, or pied cuckoo, said to subsist only on rain-drops.

[20]Un., 4.36. Viśvanātha gives two possible settings for this verse. The first is: once in private seeing Rādhā's emaciated condition, Śyāmalā affectionately begged her to eat. In responding to her, Rādhā spoke this verse. The second scenario is: Nāndīmukhī tells Rādhā, "After making numerous efforts on your behalf, it is clear that Kṛṣṇa will not meet with you. Therefore, let us think of some other way to save your life." Rādhā in the state of prior passion (*pūrva-rāga*) responds to Nāndīmukhī, who is really only testing the depth of Rādhā's love, with this verse. Prior passion is passion felt for someone before a lover has met that person face to face. Rūpa discusses it at great length in Chapter 15 of the *Blazing Sapphire*. It falls under the category of love-in-separation (*vipralambha*) since it is love felt before meeting.

अथ सुविलासा

तिर्यक्क्षिप्तचलद्दृगञ्चलरुचिर्लास्योल्लसद्भ्रूलता
कुन्दाभस्मितचन्द्रिकोज्ज्वलमुखी गण्डोच्छलत्कुण्डला ।
कन्दर्पागमसिद्धमन्त्रगहनामर्धं दुहाना गिरं
हारिण्यद्य हरेर्जहार हृदयं राधा विलासोर्मिभिः ॥४१॥

atha suvilāsā

tiryakkṣiptacaladdṛgañcalarucirlāsyollasadbhrūlatā
kundābhasmitacandrikojjvalamukhī gaṇḍocchalatkuṇḍalā |
kandarpāgamasiddhamantragahanāmardhaṃ duhānā giraṃ
hāriṇyadya harerjahāra hṛdayaṃ rādhā vilāsormibhiḥ ||41||

Her playfulness (flirtatiousness):

[*Spoken by Rūpamañjarī*[21] *to her friend. (V)*]

The beauty of her fleeting, sidelong glances,
The playful movements of her eyebrows' dances,
Her smiles, white like jasmine in bloom,
Illumine her face like light from the moon;
Her earrings flying up over her cheeks,
Her half-uttered words, invoke powers deep
Of spells from texts on the erotic arts.
Now garlanded Rādhā has Kṛṣṇa's heart—
carried on waves of amorous play.[22] (17)

---

[21]Rūpamañjarī is believed to be the name of Rūpa Gosvāmin's female identity in Kṛṣṇa's eternal sport or *līlā*. She is a younger friend/servant of Rādhā and the other friends of Rādhā in her group.

[22]Un., 4.41.

अथ महाभावपरमोत्कर्षतर्षिणी

अश्रूणामतिवृष्टिभिर्द्विगुणयन्त्यर्कात्मजानिर्झरं
ज्योत्स्नीस्यन्दिविधूपलप्रतिकृतिच्छायं वपुर्बिभ्रती ।
कण्ठान्तस्त्रुटदक्षराद्य पुलकैर्लब्धा कदम्बाकृतिं
राधा वेणुधर प्रवातकदलीतुल्या क्वचिद्वर्तते ॥४२॥

atha mahābhāvaparamotkarṣatarṣiṇī

aśrūṇāmativṛṣṭibhirdviguṇayantyarkātmajānirjharaṃ
jyotsnīsyandividhūpalapratikṛticchāyaṃ vapurbibhratī |
kaṇṭhāntastruṭadakṣarādya pulakairlabdhā kadambākṛtiṃ
rādhā veṇudhara pravātakadalītulyā kvacidvartate ||42||

Her thirsting for the highest expression of the great emotion (*mahābhāva*):

[*One of Rādhā's girlfriends speaks to Kṛṣṇa during a period of separation due to a quarrel.* (V)]

With a heavy rain of tears,
she doubles the current of
River Yamunā, Sun's Daughter;
and her body's as pale as
moonstone seen by moonlight.
Her syllables are torn in her throat,
and goosebumps sprout like *kadamba* tree[23] fruit.
Sometimes Rādhā, like a banana tree,
is shaken by the wind from a flute.[24] (18)

---

[23]The *kadamba* tree is sometimes known as the Pincushion tree.

[24]Un., 4.42. As mentioned earlier, the "great emotion" (*mahābhāva*) is considered the highest stage of *preman*, divine love or love for Kṛṣṇa. Rūpa discusses it and its various manifestations and refinements in Chapter 14 of the *Blazing Sapphire*. One of the two types of the great emotion is that in which all of the *sāttvika-bhāvas* are illuminated. It is called developed great emotion (*rūḍha-mahābhāva*). The *sāttvika-bhāvas* are outward signs of powerful inner emotion (love). They are described at length in Chapter 12 of the *Blazing Sapphire*. They are eight in number and are listed in Rūpa's previous work, *Ocean of the Nectar of Sacred Rapture* (*Brs.*, 2.3.16):

te stambha-sveda-romāñcāḥ
svarabhedo'tha vepathuḥ |
vaivarṇya maśru pralaya
ity aṣṭau sāttvikāḥ smṛtāḥ ||

Paralysis, perspiration,
horripilation, cracking of
the voice, trembling, loss of color,
tears, and fainting—these eight are
remembered as the *sāttvikas*.

Jīva says in his commentary on this verse that Rādhā is portrayed in a state of developed great emotion (*rūḍha-mahābhāva*). Viśvanātha, however, says Rādhā is in a state called *mohana-[mahābhāva]*, delusion or enchantment. This is because Rādhā, being separated from Kṛṣṇa through quarrel, was feeling love-in-separation (*viraha*). In enchantment, all of the *sāttvikas* are similarly manifest. See Un., 14.179.

अथ जगच्छ्रेणीलसद्यशाः

उत्फुल्लं किल कुर्वती कुवलयं देवेन्द्रपत्नीश्रुतौ
कुन्दं निक्षिपती विरिञ्चीगृहिणीरोमौषधीहर्षिणी ।
कर्णोत्तंससुधांशुरत्नसकलं विद्राव्य भद्राङ्गि ते
लक्ष्मीमप्यधुना चकार चकितां राधे यशःकौमुदी ॥४४॥

atha jagacchreṇīlasadyaśāḥ

utphullaṃ kila kurvatī kuvalayaṃ devendrapatnīśrutau
kundaṃ nikṣipatī viriñcīgṛhiṇīromauṣadhīharṣiṇī |
karṇottaṃsasudhāṃśuratnasakalaṃ vidrāvya bhadrāṅgi te
lakṣmīmapyadhunā cakāra cakitāṃ rādhe yaśaḥkaumudī ||44||

Her fame which shines throughout the universes:

[*Spoken by Paurṇamāsī, one of the elder ladies of the pastoral village.* (V)]

The moonlight of your fame, o fair-limbed one,
causes the blue water-lily to blossom,
offers jasmine to the ears of the
wife of Indra, king of the gods,
soothes like balm the pores of Brahmā's wife,
and has melted all the gems in the earrings
of Lakṣmī, Rādhā, and startled her![25] (19)

[25]Un., 4.44. Water-lily (*kuvalaya*) also means the earth and all the lower realms. Thus, Rādhā's fame is represented as making those blossom. As "water-lily" it also fits with the metaphor of moonlight which causes water-lilies to blossom. (V, J)

अथ गुर्वर्पितगुरुस्नेहा

न सुतासि कीर्तिदायाः किन्तु ममैवेति तथ्यमाख्यामि ।
प्राणिमि वीक्ष्य मुखं ते कृष्णस्येवेति किं त्रपसे ॥४५॥

atha gurvarpitagurusnehā

na sutāsi kīrtidāyāḥ kintu mamaiveti tathyamākhyāmi |
prāṇimi vīkṣya mukhaṃ te kṛṣṇasyeveti kiṃ trapase ||45||

Rādhā as the object of deep affection by her elders:

[*Yaśodā says this to Rādhā who stands in front of her silently with her face covered out of shyness.* (V)]

You are not the daughter of Kīrtidā
But my own. I tell you truthfully,
When I see your face, I feel love
Just like when I see Kṛṣṇa's face.
Why then do you feel such shyness?[26] (20)

[26]Un., 4.45.

अथ कृष्णप्रियावलीमुख्या, यथा ललितमाधवे (१०.१०)

सन्तु भ्राम्यदपाङ्गभङ्गिखुरलीखेलाभुवः सुभ्रुवः
स्वस्ति स्यान्मदिरेक्षणे क्षणमपि त्वामन्तरा मे कुतः ।
ताराणां निकुरम्बकेण वृतया श्लिष्टे ऽपि सोमाभया
नाकाशे वृषभानुजां श्रियमृते निष्पद्यते स्वच्छता ॥४७॥

atha kṛṣṇapriyāvalīmukhyā, yathā lalitamādhave (10.10)

santu bhrāmyadapāḍgabhaṅgikhuralīkhelābhuvaḥ subhruvaḥ
svasti syānmadirekṣaṇe kṣaṇamapi tvāmantarā me kutaḥ |
tārāṇāṃ nikurambakeṇa vṛtayā śliṣṭe 'pi somābhayā
nākāśe vṛṣabhānujāṃ śriyamṛte niṣpadyate svacchatā ||47||

Rādhā as the chief of all of Kṛṣṇa's lovers, as found in the drama *Playful Mādhava* (*Lalita-mādhava*) **(10.10):**

[*Kṛṣṇa speaks this.* (V)]

Let there be so many lovely women
with wandering, side-long glances
disposed to playful archery.
O intoxicating eyes, without you,
how can I feel good even for an instant?

Even if filled by the light of the moon
And surrounded by many groups of stars,
The sky is not luminous
Without the light of the sun of Jyeṣṭha.[27] (21)

---

[27]Un., 4.47. This verse rests on a double-entendre based on the words *vṛṣabhānujāṃ śriyaṃ* and *somābhayā*. The atmospheric side is given above. The meaning that applies to Kṛṣṇa is:

Even if embraced by Candrāvalī
Surrounded by many groups of ladies
My heart is not luminous
Without the beauty of Rādhā.

Somābhā means "light of the moon" and refers to Rādhā's chief rival for Kṛṣṇa's affection, Candrāvalī. *Vṛṣabhānujā* means the daughter of Vṛṣabhānu, i.e., Rādhā, and "born of the sun of Taurus." Taurus is the second astrological sign in the zodiac and rules from May 16 to June 16 (in Sidereal [Indic] astrology). Jyeṣṭha as the second month of the Bengali calendar, extending from the middle of May to the middle of June, corresponds with the period under the sign of Taurus. Jyeṣṭha also means "chief, best, or greatest." Kṛṣṇa is not completely happy without Rādhā present.

अथ सन्तताश्रवकेशवा

षडङ्घ्रिभिरमर्दितान्कुसुमसञ्चयानाचिनोद्
अखण्डमपि राधिके बहुशिखण्डकं त्वद्गिरा ।
अमुं च नवपल्लवव्रजमुदञ्चदर्कोज्ज्वलं
करोतु वशगो जनः किमयमन्यदाज्ञापय ॥४८॥

atha santatāśravakeśavā

ṣaḍaṅghribhiramarditānkusumasañcayānācinod
akhaṇḍamapi rādhike bahuśikhaṇḍakaṃ tvadgirā |
amuṃ ca navapallavavrajamudañcadarkojjvalaṃ
karotu vaśago janaḥ kimayamanyadājñāpaya ||48||

Rādhā as always served by Keśava (Kṛṣṇa):

[*Kṛṣṇa speaks:* (J V)]

This obedient person has
Gathered flowers unharmed by bees
And unbroken peacock feathers,
At your request, o Rādhikā,
And this bouquet of new blossoms
Illumined by the rising sun.
If there is anything else, just
Give the command and this one will do it.[28] (22)

Thus ends Chapter Four on the Rādhikā.

[28]Un., 4.48.

Leading Ladies with Kṛṣṇa

Chapter Five: Leading Ladies

नासौ नाट्ये रसे मुख्ये यत्परोढा निगद्यते ।
तत्तु स्यात्प्राकृतक्षुद्रनायिकाद्यनुसारतः ॥२॥

nāsau nāṭye rase mukhye yatparoḍhā nigadyate |
tattu syātprākṛtakṣudranāyikādyanusārataḥ ||2||

A defense of the paramour in Kṛṣṇa's sports:

That which is called adulterous love
is not acceptable as the
primary flavor (*rasa*) of a play.
But that [prohibition] should only apply
to an ordinary, small leading lady [not to the ladies of Vraja].[1]
(1)

---

[1]Un., 5.2. In support of this view, Rūpa cites a verse from a work called *The Play of Rapture* (*Rasa-vilāsa*) by an author named Sudeva. The work appears to be no longer available:

neṣṭā yadaṅgini rase kavibhir paroḍhā
tadgokulāmbujadṛśāṃ kulamantarena |
āśāṃsayā rasavidher avatāritānāṃ
kaṃsāriṇā rasikamaṇḍalaśekhareṇa ||*5.3*||

What poets don't like in the main *rasa*,
a woman married to another,
does not, however, apply to
the lotus-eyed ladies of Gokula
who were brought down by Kaṃsa's Foe [Kṛṣṇa],
the greatest of enjoyers of *rasa*,
out of a desire to relish *rasa*.

As proof that adulterous love is not ordinarily liked in the main *rasa* or flavor of a play or a poem, Jīva cites a verse from the *Sāhitya-darpaṇa* ("Mirror of Literature") by Viśvanātha Kavirāja (15th cent. CE, an Orissan author not to be confused with Viśvanātha Cakravartin 17th cent. CE.): *paroḍhāṃ varjayitvātra veśyāṃ cānanurāgiṇīm*| *ālambanaṃ nāyikā syurdakṣiṇādyāśca nāyakāḥ*||, "excluding the wife of another and the prostitute who is not attached to her clients, the supports in the erotic *rasa* are leading ladies and those leading men who are divided into the categories courteous (*dakṣiṇa*) and so forth (3.183)." But, says Jīva, this does not apply to the ladies of the cowherd village. This is so because Kṛṣṇa has caused them to descend from Goloka in order to experience a special kind of flavor (*rasa*) of love. Experiencing this flavor is the goal of the sequence of their playful actions together without regard to his omniscience, his omnipotence, or his being the lord of all. So that a particular kind of flavor (*rasa*) is possible through their mistaking themselves to be the wives of others, Kṛṣṇa causes them to forget the eternal nature of their births and sports. Therefore, the perception of themselves as married to others, and their not being sexually involved with those others is accomplished by power of sport (*līlā-śakti*).

व्रजेन्द्रनन्दनत्वेन सुष्ठु निष्ठामुपेयषुः ।
यासां भावस्य सा मुद्रा सद्भक्तैरपि दुर्गमा ॥४॥

vrajendranandanatvena suṣṭhu niṣṭhāmupeyaṣuḥ |
yāsāṃ bhāvasya sā mudrā sadbhaktairapi durgamā ||4||

The mysterious ways of lovers of Kṛṣṇa:

The special signs of love which mark
those who firmly believe
he's just the son of Vraja's chief,
are deep mysteries, even for true *bhaktas.*[2] (2)

[2]Un. 5.4. According to Viśvanātha, this verse is a response to the question of whether the ladies of Vraja desire Kṛṣṇa as the son of Vasudeva in the same way the ladies of the city (Mathurā) desire Kṛṣṇa as the son of Nanda in Vraja. The answer is no. Kṛṣṇa the son of Vasudeva represents the erotic *rasa* of marital (*dāmpatya*) love while Kṛṣṇa the son of Nanda represents to the erotic *rasa* of extra-marital (*aupapatya*) love. Kṛṣṇa is at his most attractive in the latter form. Those whose love for him has come to dwell on him in that form are not drawn to him in any other form. For them Kṛṣṇa, the son of Nanda, is the only Kṛṣṇa there is.

यथा ललितमाधवे (६.१४)

गोपीनां पशुपेन्द्रनन्दनजुषो भावस्य कस्तां कृती
विज्ञातुं क्षमते दुरूहपदवीसञ्चारिणः प्रक्रियाम् ।
आविष्कुर्वति वैष्णवीमपि तनुं तस्मिन्भुजैर्जिष्णुभिर्
यासां हन्त चतुर्भिरद्भुतरुचिं रागोदयः कुञ्चति ॥५॥

yathā lalitamādhave (6.14)

gopīnāṃ paśupendranandanajuṣo bhāvasya kastāṃ kṛtī
vijñātuṃ kṣamate durūhapadavīsañcāriṇaḥ prakriyām |
āviṣkurvati vaiṣṇavīmapi tanuṃ tasminbhujairjiṣṇubhir
yāsāṃ hanta caturbhiradbhutaruciṃ rāgodayaḥ kuñcati ||5||

For instance, in the *Playful Mādhava* (*Lalita-mādhava*) **(6.14):**

[*Rādhā, crazed by her separation from Kṛṣṇa, who had left Vṛndāvana for Mathurā, has thrown herself into the Yamunā River in Vṛndāvana and been swept to the orb of the sun. Saṃjñā, wife of the Sun god, tries to console her there by showing her the four-armed form of Viṣṇu, namely Nārāyaṇa, in the circle of the sun. It does not work. Viśākhā, who has also jumped into the river and been transported, tries to explain to the Sun's wife:* (V)]

What accomplished soul is able to know
the ways of love of village girls
for the son of the cow-herders' leader?
Their love moves down mysterious paths.
He manifests his Viṣṇu form,
but towards that, with its four all-conquering arms
and its wonderful luster—alas!—
their rising passion shrivels up.[3] (3)

[3]Un., 5.5.

यथा

रासारम्भविधौ निलीय वसता कुञ्जे मृगाक्षीगणैर्
दृष्टं गोपयितुं स्वमुद्धुरधिया या सुष्ठु सन्दर्शिता ।
राधायाः प्रणयस्य हन्त महिमा यस्य श्रिया रक्षितुं
सा शक्या प्रभविष्णुनापि हरिणा नासीच्चतुर्बाहुता ॥७॥

yathā

rāsārambhavidhau nilīya vasatā kuñje mṛgākṣīgaṇair
dṛṣṭaṃ gopayituṃ svamuddhuradhiyā yā suṣṭhu sandarśitā |
rādhāyāḥ praṇayasya hanta mahimā yasya śriyā rakṣituṃ
sā śakyā prabhaviṣṇunāpi hariṇā nāsīccaturbāhutā ||7||

Take for [another] instance:

[*Vṛndā says this to Paurṇamāsī.* (V)]

Having vanished into a bower named Vasatā
at the beginning of the Rāsa dance,
he adopted a [Viṣṇu] form with lightning wit
in order to diguise himself
when the doe-eyed ladies saw him.
Ha! Behold the greatness of Rādhā's love!
By the beauty of that alone
Hari, though all-powerful, was
unable to keep manifesting four arms.[4] (4)

---

[4]Un., 5.7. This verse is an exemplification of Rūpa's didactic statement given just before, in Un., 5.6:

bhujācatuṣṭayaṃ kvāpi narmaṇā darśayann api |
vṛndāvaneśvarīpremṇā dvibhujaḥ kriyate hariḥ ||6||

Though sometimes as a joke he [Kṛṣṇa] shows
his four arms, because of the love
of the Queen of Vṛndāvana
Hari resumes his two-armed form.

मुग्धा नववयःकामा रतौ वामा सखीवशा ।
रतिचेष्टासु सव्रीडचारुगूढप्रयत्नभाक् ॥१३॥

mugdhā navavayaḥkāmā ratau vāmā sakhīvaśā |
raticeṣṭāsu savrīḍacārugūḍhaprayatnabhāk ||13||

The innocent girl (*mugdhā*):[5]

Innocent is the girl who is
young in age and desire, indirect
in love, and controlled by her friends.
In the acts of love-making her efforts
are bashful, endearing, and secretive.[6] (5)

---

[5]The innocent girl is the first of the three varieties of herione around which most of this chapter is structured. Rūpa introduces the varieties in 5.10-11, the didactic verses before this one:

svakīyāś ca paroḍhāś ca yā dvidhā parikīrtitāḥ |
mugdhā madhyā pragalbheti pratyekaṃ tās tridhā matāḥ ||5.10||

The heroine is one of two sorts,
one's own wife and the wife of another;
of each there are three types, scholars hold:
innocent, middle, and bold-confident.

bhedatrayam idaṃ kaiścit svīyāyā eva varṇitam |
tathāpi satkavigranthe dṛṣṭatvāt tadanādṛtam ||5.11||

Some say these three types only apply
to the woman who is one's own.
Nevertheless, because all sorts of women are found
in the compositions of good poets
that view is rejected here.

Siṃhabhūpāla, for instance, is one of those who say these three qualities only belong to the wife. He says in his *Rasārṇava-sudhākara* ("Moon of the Ocean of Rasa") (1.96): *sā ca svīyā tridhā mugdhā madhyā prauḍheti kathyate*, "and she, one's own wife, may be threefold: innocent, middle, and bold-confident."

[6]Un., 5.13. Siṃhabhūpāla defines the innocent girl as follows:

mugdhā navavayaḥkāmā ratau vāmā mṛduḥ krudh i|
yatate rataceṣṭāyāṃ gūḍhaṃ lajjāmanoharam ||

Innocent is the girl who is
young in age and desire, indirect
in love, and soft in anger.
In love-making she exerts herself
secretly and with heart-stealing shyness.

Rūpa reproduces the first quarter of the stanza verbatim and the rest he paraphrases. However, his introduction of the controlling "friends" (*sakhi*) is novel here and may be Rūpa's own addition to the tradition.

कृतापराधे दयिते बाष्परुद्धावलोकना ।
प्रियाप्रियोक्तौ चाशक्ता माने च विमुखी सदा ॥१४॥

kṛtāparādhe dayite bāṣparuddhāvalokanā |
priyāpriyoktau cāśaktā māne ca vimukhī sadā ||14||

When her lover commits offense,
big tears block her gaze and she is
unable to speak dear words or harsh ones;
in her anger she turns her face away.[7] (6)

---

[7]Un., 5.14. Siṃhabhūpāla says (1.98):

kṛtāparādhe dayite vīkṣate rudatī sat ī|
apriyaṃ vā priyaṃ vāpi na kiṃcid api bhāṣate ||

When her lover commits offense
she gazes at him while crying.
She does not say anything
either harsh or dear.

Again the first quarter is verbatim, but Rūpa paraphrases the rest. Rūpa adds the idea of her turning her face away.

तत्र नववयाः

बाल्यध्वान्त सखे प्रयाहि तरसा राधावपुर्द्वीपत
स्तारुण्यद्युमणेर्यदेष विजयारम्भः पुरो जृम्भते ।
कृष्णव्योम्नि रुचिर्दरोत्तरलता ताराद्युतौ काप्युरः
पूर्वाद्रौ सुषमोन्नतिः स्मितकला पश्याद्य वक्राम्बुजे ॥१६॥

tatra navavayāḥ

bālyadhvānta sakhe prayāhi tarasā rādhāvapurdvīpata
stāruṇyadyumaṇeryadeṣa vijayārambhaḥ puro jṛmbhate |
kṛṣṇavyomni rucirdarottaralatā tārādyutau kāpyuraḥ
pūrvādrau suṣamonnatiḥ smitakalā paśyādya vaktrāmbuje ||16||

The trait of youthfulness:

[*Śyāmalā humorously describes Rādhā.* (V)]

Friend Childhood Darkness! Go quickly
from Rādhikā's island body.
The beginning of the sunrise
of her youth stands before you.
Behold now the color in the black sky,
a state of anxious trembling,
a certain restlessness in the star light,
the splendidly beautiful uplift in
the eastern mountains of her chest,
the hint of a smile on her lotus face.[8] (7)

[8]Un., 5.16.

नवकामा, यथा

बाले कंसभिदः स्मरोत्सवरसे प्रस्तूयमाने छलात्
प्रौढाभीरवधूभिरानतमुखी त्वं कर्णमध्यस्यसि ।
सव्याजं वनमालिकाविरचने ऽप्युल्लासमालम्बसे
रङ्गः को ऽयमवातरद्वद सखि स्वान्ते नवीनस्तव ॥१७॥

navakāmā, yathā

bāle kaṃsabhidaḥ smarotsavarase prastūyamāne chalāt
prauḍhābhīravadhūbhirānatamukhī tvaṃ karṇamadhyasyasi |
savyājaṃ vanamālikāviracane 'pyullāsamālambase
raṅgaḥ ko 'yamavātaradvada sakhi svānte navīnastava ||17||

Now the trait of new desire:

[*Nandīmukhī says this to Dhanyā.* (V)]

My child! When the taste of the
love games of Kaṃsa's foe[9]
are praised by more mature
village wives, you, face lowered,
perk up your ears; and pretending not to listen,
you give yourself with pleasure to
stringing garlands of wild forest flowers.
What is this new thrill that has descended
into your heart? Tell me, my friend.[10] (8)

[9]Kaṃsabhida, Kṛṣṇa.
[10]Un., 5.17.

सखीवशा

व्रजराजकुमार कर्कशे
सुकुमारीं त्वयि नार्पयाम्यमुम् ।
कलभेन्द्रकरे नवोद्यां
नलिनीं कः कुरुते जनः कृती ॥२०॥

sakhīvaśā

vrajarājakumāra karkaśe
sukumārīṃ tvayi nārpayāmyamum |
kalabhendrakare navodayāṃ
nalinīṃ kaḥ kurute janaḥ kṛtī ||20||

Being controlled by friends:

[*Lalitā talks about Rādhā to Kṛṣṇa.* (V)]

O son of the king of Vraja!
I will not offer this tender girl
to someone as roguish as you.
What sensible person
would offer a newly blossomed
lotus to the king of elephants?[11] (9)

[11]Un., 5.20. Viśvanātha comments that the point of calling Kṛṣṇa the "king of elephants" is to suggest that if he gives up his king-of-elephant character and adopts the character of a honey bee, which goes much better with lotuses, she [Lalitā] will give Rādhā to him. Lalitā is one of the chief friends of Rādhā.

सव्रीडरतप्रयत्ना, यथा

द्वित्राण्येत्य पदानि कुञ्जवसतेर्द्वारे विलासोन्मुखी
सद्यः कम्पतरङ्गदङ्गलतिका तिर्यग्विवृत्ता ह्रिया ।
भूयः स्निग्धसखीगिरां परिमलैस्तल्पान्तमासेदुषी
स्वान्तं हन्त जहार हारिहरिणीनेत्रा मम श्यामला ॥२२॥

savrīḍaratapraуatnā, yathā

dvitrāṇyetya padāni kuñjavasaterdvāre vilāsonmukhī
sadyaḥ kampataraṅgadaṅgalatikā tiryagvivṛttā hriyā |
bhūyaḥ snigdhasakhīgirāṃ parimalaistalpāntamāseduṣī
svāntaṃ hanta jahāra hāriharíṇīnetrā mama śyāmalā ||22||

Bashfulness in acts of love-making, for instance:

[*Kṛṣṇa says this to Subala the following morning.* (V)]

After coming two or three steps
in through the door of the forest cottage
looking forward to being touched,
suddenly, her vine-like body [shakes]
with wave after wave of trembles;
she turns away in bashfulness.
With the perfumes of repeated
words from her affectionate friends,
she sits on the edge of the bed.
Alas! how she's stolen my heart,
that captivating, doe-eyed lady,
that Śyāmalā of mine![12] (10)

[12]Un., 5.22.

रोषकृतबाष्पमौना, यथा

सिद्धापराधमपि शुद्धमनाः सखी मे
त्वां वक्ष्यते कथमदक्षिणमक्षमेव ।
नेमां विडम्बय कदम्बवनीभुजङ्ग
वक्त्रं पिधाय कुरुतामियमश्रुमोक्षम् ॥२३॥

roṣakṛtabāṣpamaunā, yathā

siddhāparādhamapi śuddhamanāḥ sakhī me
tvāṃ vakṣyate kathamadakṣiṇamakṣameva |
nemāṃ viḍambaya kadambavanībhujaṅga
vaktraṃ pidhāya kurutāmiyamaśrumokṣam ||23||

Silence and tears caused by anger, for instance:

[*A girlfriend of Dhanyā, who is heart-broken, speaks to Kṛṣṇa.* (V)]

Your offences have been proven.
Why then would my pure-minded friend
want to speak to double-faced you?
Don't tease her like an unbearable fool,
you serpent from the Kadamba forest!
Let her cover her face and cry![13] (11)

---

[13]Un., 5.23. Dhanyā's friend's reference to Kṛṣṇa as the "serpent of the Kadamba forest" is meant to say, "my friend Dhanyā may know who you were with last night in the Kadamba forest." (V)

तत्र समानलज्जामदना, यथा

विकिरति किल कृष्णे नेत्रपद्मं सतृष्णे
नमयति मुखमन्तःस्मेरमावृत्य राधा ।
निदधति दृशमस्मिन्नन्यतः प्रेक्षते ऽमुं
तदपि सरसिजाक्षी तस्य मोदं व्यतानीत् ॥२८॥

tatra samānalajjāmadanā, yathā

vikirati kila kṛṣṇe netrapadmaṃ satṛṣṇe
namayati mukhamantaḥsmeramāvṛtya rādhā |
nidadhati dṛśamasminnanyataḥ prekṣate 'muṃ
tadapi sarasijākṣī tasya modaṃ vyatānīt ||28||

The lady in the middle (*madhyā*, between innocent and experienced):[14]

She is both shy and passionate, for instance:

[*Nāndī says this to Paurṇamāsī.* (V)]

When Kṛṣṇa full of thirst scatters
his lotus-glances over her, Rādhā
covers her smiling face and lowers it.
When this same Kṛṣṇa casts his gaze
elsewhere, she studies him deeply.
Then, too, does the lotus-eyed lady
multiply his pleasure.[15] (12)

---

[14]Rūpa defines the "middle" lady as follows (5.27):

samānalajjāmadanā prodyattāruṇyaśālinī |
kiñcitpragalbhavacanā mohāntasuratakṣamā |
madhyā syātkomalā kvāpi māne kutrāpi karkaśā ||

Equal is she in shyness and passion;
her youthful bloom is on the rise.
Her speech is slightly more mature;
she can make love after fainting in bliss.
The middle lady may sometimes be
soft in love's spats or sometimes harsh.

Rūpa illustrates each of these features in the next set of verses. We have only included some of them here.

The first four lines of this verse, with the exception of the third quarter, are exactly the same as Siṃhabhūpāla's definition of the middle lady (1.99):

samānalajjāmadanā prodyattāruṇyaśālinī |
madhyā kāmayate kāntaṃ mohāntasuratakṣamā ||

Instead of *kiñcit-pragalbha-vacanā*, "her speech is slightly more mature," Siṃhabhūpāla has *madhyā kāmayate kāntam*, "the middle lady desires her lover."

[15]Un., 5.28.

किञ्चित्प्रगल्भोक्तिः, यथोद्धवसन्देशे (५५)

मद्वक्त्राम्भोरुहपरिमलोन्मत्त सेवानुबन्धे
पत्युः कृष्णभ्रमर कुरुषे किंतरामन्तरायम् ।
तृष्णाभिस्त्वं यदि कलरुत व्यग्रचित्तस्तदाग्रे
पुष्पैः पाण्डुच्छविमविरलैर्याहि पुंनागकुञ्जम् ॥३०॥

kiñcitpragalbhoktiḥ, yathoddhavasandeśe (55)

madvaktrāmbhoruhaparimalonmatta sevānubandhe
patyuḥ kṛṣṇabhramara kuruṣe kiṃtarāmantarāyam |
tṛṣṇābhistvaṃ yadi kalaruta vyagracittastadāgre
puṣpaiḥ pāṇḍucchavimaviralairyāhi puṃnāgakuñjam ||30||

She is somewhat more mature in speech, as in the *Tidings of Uddhava* (55):

[*Rādhā addresses this to a bumble bee.* (V)]

Intoxicated by the fragrance of
my lotus-like face, o black bee!
you are interfering
with my service to my husband.
Hey, soft-singer, if your mind
is unsettled by your appetites,
then go to the lotus bower,
whose cover is white with many flowers.[16] (13)

[16]Un., 5.30. Kṛṣṇa, who with great anticipation has been playing his flute in a garden near the house of Jaṭitā (Rādhā's mother-in-law), notices when Rādhā fails to arrive. He sends a messenger to her house to find out what has kept her, and Rādhā, being in the presence of her in-laws and unable to speak openly, speaks as if to a bumble bee who is bothering her in her work, at the same time informing the messenger of the place where she will meet Kṛṣṇa later. (V)

यथा

गोपेन्द्रनन्दन न रोदय याहि याहि
सा ते विधास्यति रुषं हृदयाधिदेवी ।
त्वन्मौलिमाल्यहृतयावकपङ्कमस्याः
पादद्वयं पुनरनेन विभूषयाद्य ॥५.४०॥

yathā

gopendranandana na rodaya yāhi yāhi
sā te vidhāsyati ruṣaṃ hṛdayādhidevī |
tvanmaulimālyahṛtayāvakapaṅkamasyāḥ
pādadvayaṃ punaranena vibhūṣayādya ||5.40||

The composed/uncomposed lady:[17]

[*Rādhā says this to Kṛṣṇa who, bowing before her, is begging her to forgive his attention to another woman.* (V)]

O Son of the king of cowherds!
Don't make me cry. Go away, go away!
She will become angry with you,
the ruling goddess of your heart.
Barley paste has been rubbed off her
by your head garland. With it you should now
decorate her two feet again.[18] (14)

[17]Rūpa after introducing the middle lady and giving examples of her traits divides her into three types, depending on how she acts in anger. He says (5.34):

tridhāsau mānavṛtteḥ syād dhīrādhīrobhayātmikā ||34||

This (middling) one is of three types
in anger: composed, uncomposed, and both.

Siṃhabhūpāla makes the same distinctions (1.100): *madhyā tridhā mānavṛtter dhīrād-hīrobhayātmikā.* The same idea is expressed here, but the wording is slightly different.

[18]Un., 5.40. Rūpa has defined the simultaneously composed and uncomposed lady in the previous verse (5.39):

dhīrādhīra tu vakroktyā sabāṣpaṃ vadati priyam ||39||

The composed/uncomposed, indeed,
With indirectness and with tears
Speaks to her beloved. (39)

Siṃhabhūpāla's next verse (1.101) defines this type of lady in exactly the same way as Rūpa: *dhīrādhīra tu vakroktyā sabāṣpaṃ vadati priyam.*

Evidence of her composure is her indirect speech, and of her lack of composure is her tears.

यथा वा

तामेव प्रतिपद्य कामवरदां सेवस्व देवीं सदा
यस्याः प्राप्य महाप्रसादमधुना दामोदरामोदसे ।
पादालक्तचितं शिरस्तव मुखं ताम्बूलशेषोज्ज्वलं
कण्ठश्चायमुरोजकुड्मलसुहृन्निर्माल्यमाल्याङ्कितः ॥५.४१॥

yathā vā

tāmeva pratipadya kāmavaradāṃ sevasva devīṃ sadā
yasyāḥ prāpya mahāprasādamadhunā dāmodarāmodase |
pādālaktacitaṃ śirastava mukhaṃ tāmbūlaśeṣojjvalaṃ
kaṇṭhaścāyamurojakuṭmalasuhṛnnirmālyamālyāṅkitaḥ ||5.41||

Again the composed/uncomposed lady:

[*Rādhā speaks angrily to Kṛṣṇa.*]

Having given yourself to her,
Who fulfills your lusty wishes,
Serve that goddess now forever!
Having achieved her great grace, now
O Dāmodara,[19] you are [surely] happy.
Your head is smeared with the lac from her feet;
Your face shines with the remnants of her *pān*;
And this neck of yours is adorned
With her used garland, dearest friend
Of the buds of her breasts.[20] (15)

---

[19]He who is bound around the belly, Kṛṣṇa

[20]Un., 5.41. The first example of the composed/uncomposed lady demonstrated the type in which self-control was greater than lack of control. This example shows lack of composure as the stronger. The lady in this example uses more bitterly ironic language than in the previous example. In the verse following this example Rūpa says this about the middle lady (5.42):

sarva eva rasotkarṣo madhyāyām eva yujyate |
yad asyāṃ vartate vyaktā maugdhyaprāgalbhyayor yutiḥ ||*42*||

All the excellence of *rasa*
is most suited for the middle one,
since in her is manifested
a union of innocence and confidence. (42)

अथ प्रगल्भा

तत्र पूर्णतारुण्या, यथा

मुष्णाति स्तनयुग्ममभ्रमुपतेः कुम्भस्थलीविभ्रमं
विस्फारं च नितम्बमण्डलमिदं रोधःश्रियं लुण्ठति ।
द्वन्द्वं लोचनयोश्च लोलशफरीविस्फूर्जितं स्पर्धते
तारुण्यामृतसम्पदा त्वमधिकं चन्द्रावलि क्षालिता ॥४४॥

atha pragalbhā

tatra pūrṇatāruṇyā, yathā

muṣṇāti stanayugmamabhramupateḥ kumbhasthalīvibhramaṃ
visphāraṃ ca nitambamaṇḍalamidaṃ rodhaḥśriyaṃ luṇṭhati |
dvandvaṃ locanayośca lolaśapharīvisphūrjitaṃ spardhate
tāruṇyāmṛtasampadā tvamadhikaṃ candrāvali kṣālitā ||44||

The boldly confident woman (*pragalbhā*).[21]

The confident woman's full bloom of youth, for instance:

[*Śrī Kṛṣṇa speaks this.* (V)]

Your two breasts steal the seductive movements
of the lobes of the Lord of Abhramu[22]
and this trembling curve of your buttock
plunders the beauty of a river bank.
Your two eyes compete with the pride
of lightning-fast fish in constant motion.
The golden nectar of youthfulness
has washed you fully, Candrāvalī.[23] (16)

---

[21]Rūpa defines the confident or bold woman in the verse before this one, 5.42:

pragalbhā pūrṇatāruṇyā madāndhoruratotsukā |
bhūribhāvodgamābhijñā rasenākrāntavallabhā |
atipraudhokticeṣṭāsau māne cātyantakarkaśā ||5.43||

Confident is she in full bloom of youth,
overthrown by pleasure, possessing a huge
desire for making love, familiar with
the rise of many states and feelings;
her lover's overcome by her selfless love (*prema-rasa*, J).
She is most bold in word and action,
and extremely harsh in anger.

In this case, Rūpa's characterization of the confident, bold woman (*pragalbhā*) differs considerably from Siṃhabhūpāla's (1.102-3):

sampūrṇayauvanonmattā pragalbhā rūḍhamanmathā |
dayitāṅge vilīneva yatate ratikeliṣu ||
rataprārambhamātre'pi gacchatyānandamūrcchanām |

"The confident woman is intoxicated by the fullness of her youth and fully accomplished in erotics; she acts in midst of love-making like she is dissolved into the body of her lover, and even at the very beginning of love-play she goes into a faint of joy."

[22]Abhramu is the female elephant of the east. Her lord is Airavata, the divine elephant of Indra. The Asian elephant has two bumps on the top of its head that in the poetic imagination of India are comparable to a woman's large breasts.

[23]Un., 5.44.

उरुरतोत्सुका, यथा

उदञ्चद्वैयात्यां पृथुनखपदाकीर्णमिथुनां
स्खलद्बर्हाकल्पां दलदमलगुञ्जामणिसराम् ।
ममानङ्गक्रीडां सखि वलयरिक्तीकृतकरां
मनस्तामेवोच्चैर्मणितरमणीयां मृगयते ॥४६॥

ururatotsukā, yathā

udañcadvaiyātyāṃ pṛthunakhapadākīrṇamithunāṃ
skhaladbarhākalpāṃ daladamalaguñjāmaṇisarām |
mamānaṅgakrīḍāṃ sakhi valayariktīkṛtakarāṃ
manastāmevoccairmaṇitaramaṇīyāṃ mṛgayate ||46||

The confident woman's great desire for making love:

[*Maṅgalā speaks this to her dear-as-life-friend (prāṇa-sakhi) in private.* (V)]

Love play, spontaneous and immodest—
in which the lovers are covered
with the marks of one another's fingernails,
with peacock feather ornaments slipping,
garlands and necklaces torn asunder,
and, O Friend, arms shorn of bracelets—
love play enhanced with soft groans and gasps—
O how intensely my heart longs for it![24] (17)

[24]Un., 5.46.

भूरिभावोद्गमाभिज्ञा

साचिप्रेङ्खदपाङ्गश्रृङ्खलशिखा विस्फारितभ्रूलता
साकूतस्मितकुड्मलावृतमुखी प्रोत्क्षिप्तरोमाङ्कुरा ।
कुञ्जे गुञ्जदलौ विराजसि चिरात्कूजद्विपञ्चीस्वरा
बद्धुं बन्धुरगात्रि कृष्णहरिणं शङ्के त्वमाकाङ्क्षसि ॥४७॥

bhūribhāvodgamābhijñā

sācipreṅkhadapāṅgaśṛṅkhalaśikhā visphāritabhrūlatā
sākūtasmitakuḍmalāvṛtamukhī protkṣiptaromāṅkurā |
kuñje guñjadalau virājasi cirātkūjadvipañcīsvarā
baddhuṃ bandhuragātri kṛṣṇahariṇaṃ śaṅke tvamākāṅkṣasi ||*47*||

The confident woman's experiencing the rise of many feelings:

[*Bakulamālā spotting Kṛṣṇa in the distance speaks this to her friend Śyāmalā who is dressed for a tryst with Kṛṣṇa.* (V)]

Your crooked glance is like the hook
At the end of a chain; wide spread
Are your eyebrows; a wishful, budding smile
Covers your face; goosebumps are on the rise;
You're aglow in your bower where bees hum.
The long-drawn notes of a lute carry far;
And, I suspect, attractive girl,
That you want to catch a black deer.[25] (18)

---

[25]Un., 5.47. Viśvanātha points out that each of these traits recognized in Śyāmalā by her friend Bakulamālā indicates a feeling. Comparing her crooked glances to hooks or lassoes suggests her wish to capture forcefully the black deer Kṛṣṇa which in turn indicates that Kṛṣṇa is late for his tryst with her, probably because he is with another woman. Those glances are expressions of Śyāmalā's envy and uncertainty. Each of the other descriptions indicates the appearance of a specific feeling. Moreover, each trait is also a method of binding Kṛṣṇa to her.

यथा

देवी नाद्य मयार्चितेति न हरे ताम्बूलमास्वादितं
शिल्पं ते परिचित्य तप्स्यति गृहीत्यङ्गी कृता न स्रजः ।
आहूतास्मि गृहे व्रजेशितुरिति क्षिप्रं व्रजन्त्या वच
स्तस्याश्रावि न भद्रयेति विनयैर्मानः प्रमाणीकृतः ॥५४॥

yathā

devī nādya mayārciteti na hare tāmbūlamāsvāditaṃ
śilpaṃ te paricitya tapsyati gṛhītyaṅgī kṛtā na srajaḥ |
āhūtāsmi gṛhe vrajeśituriti kṣipraṃ vrajantyā vaca
stasyāśrāvi na bhadrayeti vinayairmānaḥ pramāṇīkṛtaḥ ||54||

The composed confident woman (*dhīrapragalbhā*):

[*Spoken by one of Pālī's friends to her own friend.* (V)]

Bhadrā did not offer Hari betel nut
Because "I have not yet
worshipped the goddess." She refused
garlands because "My husband will
recognize your art and feel pain."
She, also, does not even listen to his words,
wandering off quickly instead, saying,
"I have been called to the house of
The Lord of Vraja!" Count it as proven
by these excuses that Bhadrā is angry.[26] (19)

---

[26]Un., 5.54. Rūpa tells us in a previous verse that like the middle woman the confident woman is of three types in anger:

mānavṛtteḥ pragalbhāpi tridhā dhīrādibhedataḥ ||*52*||

In the occurence of anger
a confident lady as well
has three varieties according to
the distinctions: composed, uncomposed, and composed/uncomposed.

Siṃhabhūpāla has the exact same wording (1.103cd): *mānavṛtteḥ pragalbhāpi tridhā dhīrādibhedataḥ.*

Rūpa defines the composed, confident woman as follows:

udāste surate dhīrā sāvahitthā ca sādarā ||*53*||

[In anger] the composed, confident lady
becomes disinterested in erotic love.
She is both respectful and
Given to dissimulation.

Siṃhabhūpāla's wording is again exactly the same (1.104ab): *udāste surate dhīrā sāvahitthā ca sādarā.* Viśvanātha remarks that the "and" (*ca*) in this verse indicates that there are two types or levels of composure intended here: complete and incomplete. Complete is indicated by disinterest in sexual love and incomplete by respect and dissimulation.

यथा वा

कुचालम्भे पाणिर्न हि मम भवत्या विघटितो
मुहुश्चुम्बारम्भे मुखमपि न साचीकृतमभूत् ।
परीरम्भे चन्द्रावलि न च वपुः कुञ्चितमिदं
क्व लब्धा मानस्य स्थितिरियमनालोकितचरी ॥५६॥

yathā vā

kucālambhe pāṇirna hi mama bhavatyā vighaṭito
muhuścumbārambhe mukhamapi na sācīkṛtamabhūt |
parīrambhe candrāvali na ca vapuḥ kuñcitamidaṃ
kva labdhā mānasya sthitiriyamanālokitacarī ||56||

Another example of the composed confident lady:

[*Kṛṣṇa says this to Candrāvalī.*]

When I place my hand on your breast,
you do not disengage it.
When I repeatedly start to kiss you,
your face does not turn away.
When I hug you, Candrāvalī,
your body does not shrink away.
Where did you get this state of anger—
something I have not seen before?[27] (20)

[27]Un., 5.56. Viśvanātha gives a little narrative introduction to this verse: "Dear Candrāvalī, are you angry with me?" "No, no, what sign of anger do you see in me? Who would be angry with someone as faultless as you?" "If this is true, will you let my touch your body?" "I will let you. What doubt could there be? This is your body." This is what she says out loud. But to herself she says: "I in my anger have given up feeling for him. But this body has been given to him. What he wants, let him have it. What have I do with him?" This indifference is a sign of the complete composure.

यथा

मुग्धाः कंसरिपो वयं रचयितुं जानीमहे नोचितं
तां नीतिक्रमकोविदां प्रियसखीं वन्देमहि श्यामलाम् ।
मल्लीदामभिरुच्छलन्मधुकरैः संयम्य कण्ठे यया
साक्षेपं चकितेक्षणस्त्वमसकृत्कर्णोत्पलैस्ताड्यसे ॥५८॥

yathā

mugdhāḥ kaṃsaripo vayaṃ racayituṃ jānīmahe nocitaṃ
tāṃ nītikramakovidāṃ priyasakhīṃ vandemahi śyāmalām |
mallīdāmabhirucchalanmadhukaraiḥ saṃyamya kaṇṭhe yayā
sākṣepaṃ cakitekṣaṇastvamasakṛtkarṇotpalaistāḍyase ||58||

The uncomposed confident lady:

[*This is spoken by Gaurī.* (V)]

Foe of Kaṃsa, we are simple women;
we would not know how to invent
anything suitable for you.
Let us praise, though, our dear friend Śyāmalā
who is well versed in proper conduct—
she restained you around your neck
with your garlands of jasmine flowers
abuzz with bees, and tauntingly
struck you with the lotuses from her ears
while you sat with fear in your eyes.[28] (21)

---

[28]Un., 5.58. Rūpa has just described the uncomposed confident lady as follows:

santarjya niṣṭhuraṃ roṣād adhīrā tāḍayet priyam ||57||

Scolding harshly out of rage,
The uncomposed lady strikes her lover.

Rūpa again uses the exact same words as Siṃhabhūpāla (1.104cd): *santarjya niṣṭhuraṃ roṣād adhīrā tāḍayet priyam.*

अथ ज्योत्स्न्यां स्वयमभिसारिका, यथा

इन्दुस्तुन्दिलमण्डलं प्रणयते वृन्दावने चन्द्रिकां
सान्द्रां सुन्दरि नन्दनो व्रजपतेस्त्वद्वीथिमुद्वीक्षते ।
त्वं चन्द्राञ्चितचन्दनेन खचिता क्षौमेण चालङ्कृता
किं वर्त्मन्यरविन्दचारुचरणद्वन्द्वं न सन्धित्ससि ॥७४॥

atha jyotsnyāṃ svayamabhisārikā, yathā

industundilamaṇḍalaṃ praṇayate vṛndāvane candrikāṃ
sāndrāṃ sundari nandano vrajapatestvadvīthimudvīkṣate |
tvaṃ candrāñcitacandanena khacitā kṣaumeṇa cālaṅkṛtā
kiṃ vartmanyaravindacārucaraṇadvandvaṃ na sandhitsasi ||74||

Among the eight situations of the heroine,[29] the lady on a tryst on a moonlit night, for instance:

[*Viśākhā says this to Rādhā.* (V)]

The moon whose circle is now full
spreads intense moonlight in Vṛndāvana.
My beauty, the son of Vraja's master
is watching the path for you.
And you, smeared with sandalwood paste,
lighted by the moon and decked with linen,
do you not wish to set your charming,
two, lotus-petal feet on the path?[30] (22)

---

[29]Rūpa now begins to describe the village ladies (*gopīs*) in terms of the eight conditions or situations of heroines from classical Sanskrit literary criticism (*alaṅkāra-śāstra*). The eight are first mentioned in the *Nāṭya-śāstra* (400 CE.), 24.210-219. They are discussed in numerous later texts as well. Siṃhabhūpāla discusses them, too (1.121-151). Here is the list Rūpa gives (5.69-70):

athāvasthāṣṭakaṃ sarvanāyikānāṃ nigadyate |
tatrābhisārikā vāsasajjā cotkaṇṭhitā tathā ||69||

khaṇḍitā vipralabdhā ca kalahāntaritāpi ca |
proṣitapreyasī caiva tathā svādhīnabhartṛkā ||70||

Next we enumerate the eight
situations of all heroines.
They are: the lady on a tryst,
the lady dressed up and ready for love,
the lady anxious to meet her lover, (69)

the lady who has been betrayed,
the lady who has been disappointed,
the lady separated by quarrel,
the lady whose lover is far away,
and the lady whose lover is
completely under her control. (70)

Rūpa's order is considerably different from that of the *Nāṭya-śāstra* and from Siṃhabhūpāla's. This might be significant, or it might be simply a matter of fitting word to meter. This stanza is an example of the trysting lady on a full moon night. The kind of clothes a lady wears on a bright, full moon night differs from what is worn on a dark, new moon night. This is a matter of camoflage. One does not want to be seen going out to meet one's lover. Rūpa's definition of the trysting lady is given in the footnote of the next verse.

[30]Un., 5.74.

तामस्यां, यथा विदग्धमाधवे (४.२२)

तिमिरमसिभिः संवीताङ्ग्यः कदम्बवनान्तरे
सखि बकरिपुं पुण्यात्मानः सरन्त्यभिसारिकाः ।
तव तु परितो विद्युद्वर्णास्तनुद्युतिसूचयो
हरि हरि घनध्वान्तान्येताः स्ववैरिणि भिन्दते ॥७५॥

tāmasyāṃ, yathā vidagdhamādhave (4.22)

timiramasibhiḥ saṃvītāṅgyaḥ kadambavanāntare
sakhi bakaripuṃ puṇyātmānaḥ sarantyabhisārikāḥ |
tava tu parito vidyudvarṇāstanudyutisūcayo
hari hari ghanadhvāntānyetāḥ svavairiṇi bhindate ||75||

The trysting lady on a dark, moonless night, an example from *Crafty Mādhava* **(***Vidagdha-mādhava,* **4.22)**

[*Lalitā speaks to Rādhā.* (V)]

Their bodies clothed in the black of darkness,
fortunate ladies go on secret visits, my friend,
with Baka's Foe[31] in the Kadamba grove.
But you? These needle-rays of your body's glow,
the color of lightning, split the darkness.

Hari! Hari! You're your own enemy.[32] (23)

---

[31]Kṛṣṇa.

[32]Un., 5.75. Rūpa defines the trysting lady as follows (5.71-72):

yābhisārayate kāntaṃ svayaṃ vābhisaratyapi |
sā jyotsnī tāmasī yānayogyaveṣābhisārikā ||71||

lajjayā svāṅgalīneva niḥśabdākhilamaṇḍanā |
kṛtāvaguṣṭhā snigdhaikasakhīyuktā priyaṃ vrajet ||72||

She invites her lover to come to her
or, goes herself to meet with him;
the trysting lady wears garments
suitable for light nights or dark. (71)

From bashfulness, her limbs together cleave;
her ornaments are silent, every one;
her head is veiled, and with her goes
one dear friend to meet her lover. (72)

यथा

रतिक्रीडाकुञ्जं कुसुमशयनीयोज्ज्वलरुचिं
वपुः सालङ्कारं निजमपि विलोक्य स्मितमुखी ।
मुहुर्ध्यायं ध्यायं किमपि हरिणा सङ्गमविधिं
समृद्ध्यन्ती राधा मदनमदमाद्यन्मतिरभूत् ॥७८॥

yathā

ratikrīḍākuñjaṃ kusumaśayanīyojjvalaruciṃ
vapuḥ sālaṅkāraṃ nijamapi vilokya smitamukhī |
muhurdhyāyaṃ dhyāyaṃ kimapi hariṇā saṅgamavidhiṃ
samṛddhyantī rādhā madanamadamādyanmatirabhūt ||78||

The lady dressed for love:

[*Watching Rādhā from afar, Rūpamañjarī speaks to her friend.* (V)]

The bower ready for erotic play,
the shining beauty of the petal bed,
and her own well ornamented body—
seeing these, a smile appears on her face.
Meditating again and yet again
Rādhā is perfecting some way
of making love with Hari, her mind
drunk with the wine of love.[33] (24)

---

[33]Un., 5.78. Rūpa defines the lady dressed for love in the following way (5.76-77):

svavāsakavaśāt kānte sameṣyati nijaṃ vapuḥ |
sajjīkaroti gehaṃ ca yā sā vāsakasajjikā ||76||

ceṣṭā cāsyāḥ smarakrīḍāsaṅkalpo vartmavīkṣaṇam |
sakhīvinodavārttā ca muhur dūtīkṣaṇādayaḥ ||77||

Because their chosen time approaches,
While her lover is yet to arrive,
She decorates her own body
And the house in which they will meet;
She is a lady dressing up for love. (76)

And her activites are these:
Imagining their love-making,
Watching the footpath for him,
Chatting with her girlfriends,
And keeping an eye out for a messenger. (77)

Rūpa's definition of this situation is very much like Siṃhabhūpala's (1.126) though not exactly the same. *svavāsakavaśāt kānte sameṣyati gṛhāntaram| sajjīkaroti cātmānaṃ yā sā vāsakasajjikā||*

My translation of *vāsaka* as "appointed or chosen day" follows Siṃhabhūpāla's discussion at 1.125cd which seems to be what Rūpa had in mind here. Jīva agrees (*svavāsakavaśāt svāvasaravaśāt*), but Viśvanātha seems confused by it and invents an unlikely and imaginative etymology for the word *vāsaka*. See the discussion of the word *vāsaka* in T. Venkatacharya's introduction to his edition of Siṃhabhūpāla's *Rasārṇavasudhākara*, cxiv-cxix, and in the notes to the verse defining *vāsaka*, 1.125cd, 54. (Madras. India: The Adyar Library and Research Centre, 1979.)

यथा

यावैर्धूमलितं शिरो भुजतटीं ताटङ्कमुद्राङ्कितां
संक्रान्तस्तनकुङ्कुमोज्ज्वलमुरो मालां परिम्लापिताम् ।
घूर्णाकुड्मलिते दृशौ व्रजपतेर्दृष्ट्वा प्रगे श्यामला
चित्ते रुद्रगुणं मुखे तु सुमुखी भेजे मुनीनां व्रतम् ॥८४॥

yathā

yāvairdhūmalitaṃ śiro bhujataṭīṃ tāṭaṅkamudrāṅkitāṃ
saṃkrāntastanakuṅkumojjvalamuro mālāṃ parimlāpitām |
ghūrṇākuḍmalite dṛśau vrajapaterdṛṣṭvā prage śyāmalā
citte rudraguṇaṃ mukhe tu sumukhī bheje munīnāṃ vratam ||84||

The lady betrayed:

[*Śyāmalā's friend Bakulamālā says this to an inquiring friend.* (V)]

His head dusted with reddish lac,
the impression of an earring
pressed into the slope of his arm,
his chest bright with kumkum powder
from a pair of encroaching breasts,
his garland of flowers flattened,
his eyes rolling and half-open—
seeing the Lord of all Vraja
in this state in the morning, Śyāmalā
raged like god Rudra in her mind
while on her face she registered good cheer
and took to silence, the vow of sages.[34] (25)

---

[34]Un., 5.84. Rūpa defines the lady betrayed in the following way (5.83):

ullaṅghya samayaṃ yasyāḥ preyān anyopabhogavān |
bhogalakṣmāṅkitaḥ prātar āgacchet sā hi khaṇḍitā |
eṣā tu roṣaniḥśvāsatūṣṇīṃbhāvādibhāg bhavet|| 83 ||

Disregarding his promised arrival time,
her lover sleeps with another.
Then, marked with signs of enjoyment,
he comes to her the next morning.
She is a lady who has been betrayed.
She displays anger, deep sighing,
and silence, among other things.

Rūpa's definition is almost exactly the same as Siṃhabhūpāla's (1.130cd-131ab): *ullaṅghya samayaṃ yasyāḥ preyān anyopabhogavān | bhogalakṣmāñcitaḥ prātar āgacchet sā hi khaṇḍhitā ||*.

यथा

स्रजः क्षिप्ता दूरे स्वयमुपहृताः केशिरिपुणा
प्रियवाचस्तस्य श्रुतिपरिसरान्ते ऽपि न कृताः ।
नमन्नेष क्षौणीविलुठितशिखं प्रैक्षि न मया
मनस्तेनेदं मे स्फुटति पुटपाकार्पितमिव ॥८८॥

yathā

srajaḥ kṣiptā dūre svayamupahṛtāḥ keśiripuṇā
priyavācastasya śrutiparisarānte 'pi na kṛtāḥ |
namanneṣa kṣauṇīviluṭhitaśikhaṃ praikṣi na mayā
manastenedaṃ me sphuṭati puṭapākārpitamiva ||88||

The lady separated by quarrel:

[*Śrī Rādhā says this to herself.* (V)]

The garlands have been tossed far away,
the ones brought by Keśi's Adversary.[35]
His dear words I did not allow
anywhere near the edges of my ears.
Nor as he bowed, his peacock crown
rolling on the ground, did I look at him.
Because of that, this heart of mine
Feels like it's in a cheap clay pot.[36] (26)

---

[35]Keśiripu, i.e. Kṛṣṇa.

[36]Un., 5.88. Rūpa defines the lady separated from her lover by quarrel in this way (5.87):

yā sakhīnāṃ puraḥ pādapatitaṃ vallabhaṃ ruṣā |
nirasya paścāt tapati kalahāntaritā hi sā |
asyāḥ pralāpasantāpaglāniniḥśvasitādayaḥ ||*87*||

In front of her friends, she, out of anger,
drives away her lover who has bowed down
at her feet. Later she torments herself.
Such a lady is distanced by quarrel.
She laments, sorrows, languishes,
sighs deeply and so forth.

Siṃhabhūpāla's (1.132cd-133ab) definition is: *yā sakhīnāṃ puraḥ pādapatitaṃ vallabhaṃ ruṣā*| *nirasya paścāt tapati kalahāntaritā tu sā*||. Siṃhabhūpāla gives more of the typical actions of a lady in this situation. He includes being mistaken, confused, and having fevers (1.133cd-134ab).

यथा

विलासी स्वच्छन्दं वसति मथुरायां मधुरिपु
र्वसन्तः सन्तापं प्रथयति समन्तादनुपदम् ।
दुराशेयं वैरिण्यहह मदभीष्टोद्यमविधौ
विधत्ते प्रत्यूहं किमिह भविता हन्त शरणम् ॥९०॥

yathā

vilāsī svacchandaṃ vasati mathurāyāṃ madhuripu
rvasantaḥ santāpaṃ prathayati samantādanupadam |
durāśeyaṃ vairiṇyahaha madabhīṣṭodyamavidhau
vidhatte pratyūhaṃ kimiha bhavitā hanta śaraṇam ||90||

The lady whose lover is abroad:

[*Śrī Rādhā says this to Lalitā.* (V)]

The Foe of Madhu[37] happily
lives in Mathurā of his own free will.
Spring spreads despair all around with each step I take.
Aeiii! This vain hope[38] is my enemy!
It blocks my efforts to achieve my desired end [ending my life].
Ah! What will be my refuge now?[39] (27)

[37]Madhuripu, Kṛṣṇa.
[38]That he will come back.
[39]Un., 5.90. Rūpa defines the lady whose lover is abroad as follows (5.89):

dūradeśaṃ gate kānte bhavet proṣitabhartṛkā |
priyasaṃkīrtanaṃ dainyam asyās tānavajāgarau |
mālinyam anavasthānaṃ jāḍyacintādayo matāḥ ||89||

When her lover has gone
to a far distant place,
she becomes a lady
whose lover is abroad.
She praises her lover, feels depression
wastes away, cannot sleep, forgets to wash,
becomes unsteady, dull,
and given to worry. (89)

Siṃhabhūpāla's definition of the lady whose lover is away is (1.123): *dūradeśaṃ gate kānte bhavet proṣitabhartṛkā | asyās tu jāgaraḥ kārśyam nimittādivilokanam ||*, "when her lover has gone to a distant place, she becomes a lady whose lover is abroad. She remains awake [at night], becomes thin [from not eating properly], and watches for signs and omens [of her lover's fortune or return]."

यथा

मुदा कुर्वन्पत्राङ्कुरमनुपमं पीनकुचयोः
श्रुतिद्वन्द्वे गन्धाहृतमधुपमिन्दीवरयुग्मम् ।
सखेलं धम्मिल्लोपरि च कमलं कोमलमसौ
निराबाधां राधां रमयति चिरं केशिदमनः ॥९२॥

yathā

mudā kurvanpatrāṅkuramanupamaṃ pīnakucayoḥ
śrutidvandve gandhāhṛtamadhupamindīvarayugmam |
sakhelaṃ dhammillopari ca kamalaṃ komalamasau
nirābādhāṃ rādhāṃ ramayati ciraṃ keśidamanaḥ ||92||

The lady who controls her lover:

[*Vṛndā says this to Paurṇamāsī.* (V)]

With pleasure he draws matchless leaves and shoots
on her golden breasts, and then on her ears
he places blue lotuses whose fragrance
draws honey-drinking bees. And next, trembling,
He binds a soft lotus at the crown of
her braided hair. The Crusher of Keśi[40]
forever brings placid Rādhā delight.[41] (28)

---

[40]Keśidamana, Kṛṣṇa.

[41]Un., 5.92. Rūpa defines the lady who controls her lover (*svādhīnabhartṛkā*) as follows (5.91):

> *svāyattāsannadayitā bhavet svādhīnabhartṛkā |*
> *salilāraṇyavikrīḍākusumāvacayādikṛt ||91||*
>
> When her dear sits nearby, under her control,
> she's the lady who's conquered her lover.
> She loves him in flood and in forest
> And sends him to gather flowers.

Siṃhabhūpāla's definition is (1.150): *svāyattāsannapatikā hṛṣṭā svādhīnavallabhā | asyās tu ceṣṭāḥ kathitāḥ smarapūjāmahotsavaḥ || vanakelijalakrīḍākusumāpacayādayaḥ*, "She whose lover sits nearby under her control is thrilled. She's conquered her lover. Her activities are called a great festival in worship of erotic love. Those activities are dallying in the forest, frisking in the waters, collecting flowers, and so forth."

यथा वा, श्रीगीतगोविन्दे (१२.२५)

रचय कुचयोश्चित्रं पत्रं कुरुष्व कपोलयो
र्घटय जघने काञ्चीमञ्च स्रजा कवरिभरम् ।
कलय वलयश्रेणीं पाणौ पदे कुरु नूपुरा-
विति निगदितः प्रीतः पिताम्बरो ऽपि तथाकरोत् ॥९३॥

yathā vā, śrīgītagovinde (12.25)

racaya kucayościtraṃ patraṃ kuruṣva kapolayo
rghaṭaya jaghane kāñcīmañca srajā kavaribharam |
kalaya valayaśreṇīṃ pāṇau pade kuru nūpurā-
viti nigaditaḥ prītaḥ pitāmbaro 'pi tathākarot ||93||

Or, the lady who controls her lover in the *Song of Govinda* **(***Gīta-govinda***) (12.25):**

"Draw leaves on my breasts; decorate
my cheeks; fix my gem girdle on my thighs;
wind my fine hair with a garland;
attach my bracelets to my arms;
place my ankle bells on my feet."
Pleased to be spoken to like this,
Yellow-robed Kṛṣṇa did just what she asked.[42] (29)

[42]This stanza from Jayadeva's (12th cent. CE) *Gītagovinda* (*The Song of Govinda*) is cited at Un., 5.93.

तत्र उत्तमा, यथा

कर्तुं शर्म क्षणिकमपि मे साध्यमुज्झत्यशेषं
चित्तोत्सङ्गे न भजति मया दत्तखेदाप्यसूयाम् ।
श्रुत्वा चान्तर्विदलति मृषाप्यार्तिवार्तालवं मे
राधा मूर्धन्यखिलसुदृशां राजते सद्गुणेन ॥९८॥

tatra uttamā, yathā

kartuṃ śarma kṣaṇikamapi me sādhyamujjhatyaśeṣaṃ
cittotsaṅge na bhajati mayā dattakhedāpyasūyām |
śrutvā cāntarvidalati mṛṣāpyārtivārtālavaṃ me
rādhā mūrdhanyakhilasudṛśāṃ rājate sadguṇena ||98||

Among the three levels of lady, the highest:[43]

[*Kṛṣṇa says this to his friend Subala.* (V)]

To do even a moment's good for me
she gives up countless of her own projects.
Though I give her distress, in the bottom
of her heart she does not feel displeasure.
Hearing even a false rumor
of my injury, her heart splits apart.
Rādhā with her virtues stands at the head
Of all lovely women.[44] (30)

Thus ends Chapter Five on the Leading Ladies.

---

[43]Rūpa submits one last way of classifying the ladies who love Kṛṣṇa: highest, middling, and lowest. These classifications are based on the fullness of their love (*preman*) for him. Rūpa says in a previous verse (5.96):

uttamā madhyamā cātra kaniṣṭhā ceti tāstridhā |
vrajendranandane prematāratamyena kīrtitāḥ ||96||

They are known to be of three types:
The highest, middling, and lowest,
According to the degree of their love
For the son of the King of Vraja. (96)

Siṃhabhūpāla also recognizes these three types (1.151cd), but connects them to the depth of their love for their lovers, not for Kṛṣṇa: *uttamā madhyamā nīcety evaṃ sarvāḥ striyas tridhā.* Siṃhabhūpāla gives fuller definitions than Rūpa does for these three types (1.152-157).

[44]Un., 5.98.

Group Leaders

Chapter Six: Faction Leaders

तत्र आत्यन्ताधिका, यथा

तावद्भद्रा वदति चटुलं फुल्लतामेति पाली
शालीनत्वं त्यजति विमला श्यामलाहङ्करोति ।
स्वैरं चन्द्रावलिरपि चलत्युन्नमय्योत्तमाङ्गं
यावत्कर्णे न हि निविशते हन्त राधेति मन्त्रः ॥७॥

tatra ātyantādhikā, yathā

tāvadbhadrā vadati caṭulaṃ phullatāmeti pālī
śālīnatvaṃ tyajati vimalā śyāmalāhaṅkaroti |
svairaṃ candrāvalirapi calatyunnamayyottamāṅgaṃ
yāvatkarṇe na hi niviśate hanta rādheti mantraḥ ||7||

The absolutely superior lady:

[*Once when the village women were gathered together and conversations about who was the best among them had begun with each one deceitfully praising the good fortune of her own group, Śyāmalā spoke up saying, "Listen, o ladies of Vraja, to the real truth." She then said this to them:* (V)]

Bhadrā flatters, Pālī blossoms,
Vimalā gives up her shyness,
Śyāmalā becomes arrogant,
Even Candrāvalī wanders about
Freely, raising her head up high,
As long as, that is, the *mantra* "Rā-dhā"
Does not enter into their ears.[1] (1)

---

[1]Un., 6.7. Among the ladies of Vraja there are many groups or factions and among them some factions are led by bold, outspoken women and some by shy or reserved women. Rūpa defines the "absolute superior" faction leader in the following way in the previous verse (6.6):

sarvathaivāsamordhā yā sā syād ātyantikādhikā |
sā rādhā sā tu madhyaiva yan nānyā sadṛśī vraje ||6||

Unequaled or surpassed in all respects,
completely superior is she.
Such a one is Rādhā.
But she is a middle lady.
No one else is like her in Vraja.

Rādhā's being a middle lady (*madhyā*) here means she is midway between the hard or bold lady (*prakharā*) and the soft or pliant lady (*mṛdvī*).

अथ अधिकमध्या

आलीभिर्मे त्वमसि विदिता पूर्णिमाया प्रदोषे
रोषेणासौ प्रथयसि कथं पाटवेनावहित्थाम् ।
धृत्वा धूर्ते सहपरिजनां मद्गृहे त्वां निरुन्ध्यां
वर्त्मप्रेक्षी गुणयतु स ते जागरं कुञ्जराजः ॥१०॥

atha adhikamadhyā

ālībhirme tvamasi viditā pūrṇimāyā pradoṣe
roṣeṇāsau prathayasi kathaṃ pāṭavenāvahitthām |
dhṛtvā dhūrte sahaparijanāṃ madgṛhe tvāṃ nirundhyāṃ
vartmaprekṣī guṇayatu sa te jāgaraṃ kuñjarājaḥ ||10||

The relatively superior poised lady:[2]

[*Kṛṣṇa has gone to a trysting place. Hearing this from a messenger, some lady of Vraja spots another lady on her way to that bower dressed in white clothes suitable for moving about unnoticed on a moonlit night. She addresses her as follows:*]

I know you and your friends.
Why do you with your cleverness
on this evening of the full moon
try to hide who you are from me?
Out of anger perhaps I will
catch you along with your friends
and hold you captive in my house.
Let that king of the bower spend the night
awake watching the path for you.[3] (2)

---

[2]Rūpa defines the relatively superior faction leader as follows (6.8):

madhye yūthādhināthānām apekṣyaikatamām iha |
yā syād anyatamā śreṣṭhā sā proktāpekṣikādhikā ||8||

Among the leaders of the factions,
By comparison to one girl
Another girl who is better
Is called relatively superior.

As with the leading ladies described in the last chapter, the relatively superior faction leaders are either bold (*prakharā*), poised (*madhyā*), or retiring (*mṛdu*).

[3]Un., 6.10. According to Viśvanātha, the lady who is addressed here is the proper example of the superior middle lady. Since she is on her way to meet Kṛṣṇa, she has greater good fortune than the lady addressing her, who is not. Since she is trying to hide her movements, she is not bold (*prakharā*). Since she exhibits cleverness in disguising herself she is not retiring or unaggressive (*mṛdu*). She is thus a superior poised woman. The woman who is addressing her is a different sort. Since she threatens to capture her, she is bold. And since nothing indicates she has had the good fortune of meeting with Kṛṣṇa, she is a less-gifted (*laghu*) lady. She is thus a bold, but less-gifted woman (*laghu-prakharā*) and she is not a friend of the lady addressed.

अथ अधिकमृद्वी

न्यञ्चन्मूर्धा सह परिजनैर्दूरतो मा प्रयासी-
र्मामालोक्य प्रियसखि यतः प्रेमपात्री ममासि ।
माला मौलौ तव परिचिता मत्कलाकौशलाढ्या
द्यूते जित्वा दनुजदमनं या त्वया स्वीकृतास्ति ॥११॥

atha adhikamṛdvī

nyañcanmūrdhā saha parijanairdūrato mā prayāsī-
rmāmālokya priyasakhi yataḥ premapātrī mamāsi |
mālā maulau tava paricitā matkalākauśalāḍhyā
dyūte jitvā danujadamanaṃ yā tvayā svīkṛtāsti ||11||

The relatively superior timid faction leader:

[*After making love with Kṛṣṇa, some beauty of Vraja while walking on the path to her home with her friends realized she had been spotted from afar. In embarrassment she was trying to make an escape. The lady who spotted her, a superior soft lady [in her faction], said this to her with affection:* (VG)]

Don't leave after spotting me from afar,
with your companions and your head bent down!
Dear friend, you are someone I love.
I recognize that garland in your hair.
It has the markings of my skillful art.
I am sure you won it by beating
the Subduer of Danuja[4]
at a game of dice.[5] (3)

[4]Danujadamana, Kṛṣṇa

[5]Un., 6.11. Viśvanātha thinks, contra Viṣṇudāsa Gosvāmin, that it is the lady who is addressed who is the example of the superior timid lady, not the speaker. He thinks the speaker is a less-gifted, but poised member of her faction (*laghu-madhyā*) who is a friend of the lady addressed.

तत्र समप्रखरा

न भवति तव पार्श्वे चेत्सखी कापि माभूत्
परिहर हृदि कम्पं किं हरिस्ते विधाता ।
अहमतिचतुराभिर्वेष्टितालीघटाभिः
प्रियसखि पुरतस्ते दुस्तरा बाहुदास्मि ॥१३॥

tatra samaprakharā

na bhavati tava pārśve cetsakhī kāpi mābhūt
parihara hṛdi kampaṃ kiṃ hariste vidhātā |
ahamaticaturābhirveṣṭitālīghaṭābhiḥ
priyasakhi purataste dustarā bāhudāsmi ||13||

Equal bold ladies:[6]

[*The leaders of two factions were collecting flowers in Kṛṣṇa's grove. Kṛṣṇa spotted them from afar, and asking himself repeatedly "who is cutting flowers in my grove?" came running towards them. Seeing that, the softer lady cutting the flowers became frightened. In order to reassure her a bolder friend said:*]

If there were no friend at your side
would you then not have any fear?
Give up that trembling in your heart.
What? Is Hari your creator?
I, along with these very clever friends,
am in front of you, sweet friend,
a river Bāhudā[7] hard to cross over.[8] (4)

---

[6]Rūpa describes equality as follows (6.12):

sāmyaṃ bhaved adhikayos tathā laghuyugasya ca ||12||

Equality may exist between
Two superior ladies and two less-gifted ladies.

There are three varieties of equal ladies as well: bold, poised, and timid.

[7]Bāhudā, also means a giver of arms [to fend Kṛṣṇa off].

[8]Un., 6.13. Since both ladies are the objects of Kṛṣṇa's attention, they are equal.

अथ सममध्या

लोले न स्पृश मां तवालिकतटे धातुर्यदालक्ष्यते
त्वं स्पृश्यासि कथं भुजङ्गरमणी दूरादतस्त्यज्यसे ।
धिग्वामं वदसि त्वमेव कुहकप्रेष्ठासि भोगाङ्किते
येनाद्य च्युतकञ्चुकाः शुषिर् अतःसख्योऽपि सर्पन्ति ते ॥१४॥

atha samamadhyā

lole na spṛśa māṃ tavālikataṭe dhāturyadālakṣyate
tvaṃ spṛśyāsi kathaṃ bhujaṅgaramaṇī dūrādatastyajyase |
dhigvāmaṃ vadasi tvameva kuhakapreṣṭhāsi bhogāṅkite
yenādya cyutakañcukāḥ śuṣir ataḥsakhyo'pi sarpanti te ||14||

Equal poised ladies:

[*This verse consists of a dialog between two faction leaders who are friends, both equally lovers of Kṛṣṇa, having some witty fun with each other.*]

"Restless girl, don't touch me since
on the side of your forehead
some reddish substance is showing."[9]

"How is it you think you are touchable?
You are the lover of a snake
and thus are to be kept at a distance."[10]

"Shame! You speak the reverse of the truth.
You are the dearest of the snake,
covered by marks of enjoyment,
because of which, now, charmed by the flute
even your friends have sloughed off their skins
and are rising up like serpents."[11] (5)

---

[9]Therefore, you have been enjoyed by Kṛṣṇa and are impure. (V)

[10]You are a well-known lover of Kṛṣṇa and are the initiator of such love-making. I, however, was taken by him by force and was enjoyed without wishing it. Therefore, you are much more impure than me. (V)

[11]Un., 6.14. That is, your breasts have come out of your blouse and are rising up in excitement.

यथा वा

प्रहित्य कठिने निजं परिजनं मदार्या त्वया
निकामम् उपजप्यतां किमु विभीषिकाडम्बरैः ।
व्रजामि रविजातटे गुरुगिरा मृषाशङ्किनि
प्रदोषसमये समं सवयसा शिवां सेवितुम् ॥ १६ ॥

yathā vā

prahitya kaṭhine nijaṃ parijanaṃ madāryā tvayā
nikāmam upajapyatāṃ kimu vibhīṣikāḍambaraiḥ |
vrajāmi ravijātaṭe gurugirā mṛṣāśaṅkini
pradoṣasamaye samaṃ savayasā śivāṃ sevitum ||16||

Again, equal poised ladies:

[*This is spoken by a bold lady to a timid lady who asked, "Pretty woman, are you not afraid of your elders, since in the evening you clearly go to the forest?"* (V)]

Send one of your companions, cruel girl,
To my elders and whisper all you want.
What do I care for your frightening noise?
I go to the bank of the Yamunā
By the order of my elders
Every evening, you fake doubter,
With a friend, to serve Śiva's wife.[12] (6)

[12]Un., 6.16

अथ लघुमध्या

गोष्ठाधीशसुतस्य सा नवनवप्रेष्ठस्य यावद्दृशोः
पन्थानं वृषभान्जा सखि वशीकारौषधिज्ञा ययौ ।
तावत्त्वय्यपि रूक्षमस्य बलवद्दाक्षिण्यमेवेक्ष्यते
का चन्द्रावलि देवि दुर्भगतया दूनात्मनां नः कथा ॥२०॥

atha laghumadhyā

goṣṭhādhīśasutasya sā navanavapreṣṭhasya yāvaddṛśoḥ
panthānaṃ vṛṣabhānjā sakhi vaśīkārauṣadhijñā yayau |
tāvattvayyapi rūkṣamasya balavaddākṣiṇyameveksyate
kā candrāvali devi durbhagatayā dūnātmanāṃ naḥ kathā ||20||

The relatively less-gifted but poised lady:[13]

[*This is addressed to Candrāvalī by a less-gifted but poised lady.*]

As long as the eyes of the son
of the lord of the pasture—
who's known for taking new lovers—
have Vṛṣabhānu's daughter, Rādhā, before them—
who knows herbs to control people—
his passion, even for you
becomes whithered, Candrāvalī.
What can be said about us, good lady,
who are afflicted by bad luck?[14] (7)

---

[13]Rūpa informs us that there are two types of less-gifted leader, relative and absolute (6.17):

> *laghurāpekṣikī cātyantikī ceti dvidhoditā ||17||*
>
> The less-gifted lady is of two types:
> The relative and absolute.

Then he defines the relatively less-gifted faction leader (6.18):

> *madhye yūthādhināthānām apekṣyaikatamām iha|*
> *yā syādanyatamā nyūnā sā proktāpekṣikī laghuḥ ||18||*
>
> Among the leaders of factions,
> by comparison to one lady
> another lady who is less fortunate
> is called relatively less-gifted.

The relatively less-gifted faction leader is again of three types: bold, poised, or timid. By "gifted" he means gifted with Kṛṣṇa's favor.

[14]Un., 6.20.

अथ लघुमृद्वी

अपसरणमितो नः सांप्रतं सांप्रतं स्या-
द्यदपि हरिचकोरं चित्रमालोचयामः ।
कलयत सहचर्यः पर्यटद्गौरदीप्ति-
स्तटभुवि नवशोभां सौति चन्द्रावलीयम् ॥२१॥

atha laghumṛdvī

apasaraṇamito naḥ sāṃpratam sāṃpratam syā-
dyadapi haricakoram citramālocayāmaḥ |
kalayata sahacaryaḥ paryaṭadgauradīpti-
staṭabhuvi navaśobhāṃ sauti candrāvalīyam ||*21*||

The relatively less-gifted timid lady:

Our departure from here now is fitting,
though we are viewing the wonderful
cakora bird, Hari. But look, my friends!
This Candrāvalī's golden glow
spreads all around. She infuses
this river bank with a new loveliness.[15] (8)

[15]Un., 6.21.

यथा

निजनिखिलसखीनामाग्रहेणाघवैरी
कथमपि स मयाद्य व्यक्तमामन्त्रितोऽस्ति ।
क्षणमुरुकरुणाभिः संवरीतुं त्रपां मे
मदुदवसितलक्ष्मीं गोष्ठदेव्यस्तनुध्वम् ॥२३॥

yathā

nijanikhilasakhīnāmāgraheṇāghavairī
kathamapi sa mayādya vyaktamāmantrito'sti |
kṣaṇamurukaruṇābhiḥ saṃvarītuṃ trapāṃ me
madudavasitalakṣmīṃ goṣṭhadevyastanudhvam ||23||

The absolutely less-gifted faction leader:[16]

[*The foe of Agha, Kṛṣṇa, was invited on my birthday today. I told him: "though you have been invited and fed at the celebration hosted by my parents, come to my bower this evening to eat something." But, my friends, since he is submissive to you, without your help my heart's desire will not be fulfilled.* (V)]

Encouraged by all my friends,
I have somehow openly invited
to my house Agha's foe, Kṛṣṇa.
To hide my bashfulness for a moment,
o village ladies, with your great compassion,
please increase the loveliness of my house.[17] (9)

Thus ends Chapter Six on the Group Leaders.

---

[16]Rūpa defines the absolutely less-gifted faction leader as follows (6.22):

anyā yato'sti na nyūnā sā syādātyantikī laghuḥ |
traividhyasambhave'pyasyā mṛdutaivocitā bhavet ||

She than whom no one is less fortunate
is the absolutely least gifted lady.
Though three varieties are possible,
Timid alone is suitable.

[17]Un., 6.23.

The Messengers

Chapter Seven: The Messengers

तत्र स्वार्थयाञ्चया शब्दोत्थो व्यङ्ग्यो, यथा

पुष्पमार्गणमनोरथोद्धता
कृष्ण मञ्जुलतया तवानया ।
रक्षितास्मि सविकासया पुरो
विस्फुरत्सुमनसं कुरुष्व माम् ॥१३॥

tatra svārthayācñayā śabdottho vyaṅgyo, yathā

puṣpamārgaṇamanorathoddhatā
kṛṣṇa mañjulatayā tavānayā |
rakṣitāsmi savikāsayā puro
visphuratsumanasaṃ kuruṣva mām ||13||

An example of suggestion by word through petition or request on one's own behalf:[1]

[*Rādhā says this to Kṛṣṇa:*]

Filled with a wish to gather flowers,
Kṛṣṇa, I'm arrested by this
your beautiful blossoming vine
before me. Make me possessor
of shimmering, lovely flowers.[2] (1)

---

[1]The messenger is a very important link connecting the village ladies with Kṛṣṇa. Messaging can be achieved through a trusted friend or helper, or, a lady can act as her own messenger, using her speech and gestures with her body or eyes to invite Kṛṣṇa's attention. Speech here means words used suggestively (*vyaṅgya*), operating either through the power of the word itself or its meaning. Here suggestion is delivered through the word itself by means of petition.

[2]Un., 7.13. Kṛṣṇa responds to Rādhā's request by gathering flowers himself and slipping them inside her blouse. (V) The force of the words chosen for use here suggests another, more amorous message. It can be expressed in this way:

Stirred up by a wish for eros,
Kṛṣṇa, I am captured by this
your blossoming beauty before
me. Make me one whose heart is thrilled
with bursting erotic pleasure.

अर्थोत्थो, यथा

वृन्दारण्यं भुजगनिकराक्रान्तमश्रान्तमस्मात्
कात्यायन्यै कुसुमपटलीं जातभीर्नाहरामि ।
तेन क्रीडोद्धूतफणिपते श्रद्धयास्मि प्रपन्ना
त्वामेकान्ते दिश विषहरं मन्त्रमेकं प्रसीद ॥१४॥

arthottho, yathā

vṛndāraṇyaṃ bhujaganikarākrāntamaśrāntamasmāt
kātyāyanyai kusumapaṭalīṃ jātabhīrnāharāmi |
tena krīḍoddhūtaphaṇipate śraddhayāsmi prapannā
tvāmekānte diśa viṣaharaṃ mantramekaṃ prasīda ||14||

Now, an example of suggestion by meaning through petition on one's own behalf:

The forest of Vṛndā
is overrun by countless snakes.
Because of this, fearful,
I am not gathering flowers
for the goddess Kātyāyanī.
Therefore, lord who plays on raised hoods,[3]
I, in this lonely place,
approach you, faithfully.
Teach me a *mantra* that removes poison.[4] (2)

---

[3]This is a reference to Kṛṣṇa's dancing on the hoods of the serpent Kāliya in the river Yamunā in order to drive the snake away and make the river safe for use by the villagers. See Bhāg. 10.16.

[4]Un., 7.14. Kṛṣṇa responds: "one should not pronounce a *mantra* loudly. Bring your right ear close to my mouth." When she does, under the guise of giving her a *mantra* he kisses her cheek and removes her blouse for his fees. Her reference to a *mantra* that removes poison suggests that she has already been bitten by the snake of passion. (V)

अर्थोत्थो, यथा

असूर्यंपश्यापि प्रियसहचरीप्रेमभिरहं
तवाभ्यर्णं लब्ध्वा मधुमथन दूत्यं विदधती ।
द्रुतं तस्याः स्नेहं निशमय न यावच्छशिधिया
धयन्वक्त्रज्योत्स्नां निशि हतचकोरस्तुदति माम् ॥१७॥

arthottho, yathā

asūryaṃpaśyāpi priyasahacarīpremabhirahaṃ
tavābhyarṇaṃ labdhvā madhumathana dūtyaṃ vidadhatī |
drutaṃ tasyāḥ snehaṃ niśamaya na yāvacchaśidhiyā
dhayanvaktrajyotsnāṃ niśi hatacakorastudati mām ||17||

Now, an example of a request on behalf of oneself in the guise of a request on behalf of another. This effect is produced by meaning:

Though I am one who never sees the sun,
out of love for my dearest friend
I have come to you, stirrer of Madhu,
carrying a message from her.
Quickly hear of her affection
before that accursed *cakora*,
mistaking the glow of my face
in the night for the moon, strikes me.[5] (3)

---

[5]Un., 7.17. Kṛṣṇa replies: "Then I will hear of her affection for me later. First, I am thinking of a way to protect *you*. If you remain standing here outside, this wicked *cakora* will not let you be. Right here is a mountain cave filled with complete darkness, but you will be afraid to enter it by yourself. Therefore, I will hide you here on my chest for a few moments and deceive that *cakora*. Then I can hear about her affection." The suggested meanings here are: since I am not seen in the sun, seeing me is rare, and since my face is mistaken for the moon, I am beautiful and sweet. In other words I am worthy of your enjoyment, Kṛṣṇa. (V)

तेन शब्दोत्थो, यथा

त्यजन्कुवलयाधिकां घनरसश्रियोल्लासिनीं
पुरः सुरतरङ्गिणीं मधुरमत्तहंसस्वनाम् ।
मलीमसपयोधरामपि मदान्धे पद्मिन्निमां
भजन्किमिव पङ्किलामहह कर्मनाशामपि ॥१९॥

tena śabdottho, yathā

tyajankuvalayādhikāṃ ghanarasaśriyollāsinīṃ
puraḥ surataraṅgiṇīṃ madhuramattahaṃsasvanām |
malīmasapayodharāmapi madāndhe padminnimāṃ
bhajankimiva paṅkilāmahaha karmanāśāmapi ||19||

Suggestion through pretext produced by word:

[*This is spoken by some outspoken lady to Kṛṣṇa, who is looking at another lady who is her competitor.* (V)]

Rejecting the river of gods
before you, richer in water-lilies,
fuller of tumbling waters,
resonant with honey-drunken geese,
O intoxicant-blinded elephant,
do you instead turn to that muddy stream,
though it destroys good deeds
and bears dirty waters?[6] (4)

---

[6]Un., 7.19. The word for "river of gods" if divided differently means "one who takes pleasure in making love." "Richer in water-lilies" divided differently means "greatest in the world." "Fuller of tumbling waters" means "radiant with the beauty of erotic rapture." Finally, the mention of "before you" prompts Kṛṣṇa to respond with only a side glance which means, "Then enter the bower before us." One could reword the verse to apply this suggested meaning:

Rejecting one passionate
in love-making, best in the world,
radiant with the beauty of
erotic rapture, whose ankle-bells
sound like sweet and drunken geese,
and who is right here before you,
o holder of the sport-lotus,
blinded by wantonness, do you
instead turn to her, destroyer
of clever actions, whose breasts are
impure, and who is sinful?

तत्र शब्दोत्थो, यथा

आहूयमानास्मि कथं त्वयालिनां
स्वनैः स्वपुष्पावचयाय मालति ।
आमोदपूर्णं सुमनोभिराश्रितं
पुन्नागमेव प्रमदेन कामये ॥२२॥

tatra śabdottho, yathā

āhūyamānāsmi kathaṃ tvayālināṃ
svanaiḥ svapuṣpāvacayāya mālati |
āmodapūrṇaṃ sumanobhirāśritaṃ
punnāgameva pramadena kāmaye ||22||

Suggestion produced by word when the subject is nearby:[7]

Why am I being hailed by you,
o Jasmine, to collect *your* blooms
through the soft buzzing of the bees?
I desire with delight the white lotus,
full of fragrance and beautiful blossoms.[8] (5)

---

[7]This kind of verbal suggestion occurs when the intended hearer is present, but is not the one being directly spoken to. In the previous examples Kṛṣṇa was directly addressed suggestively. Here others are addressed, but with a suggestive message for Kṛṣṇa. This is called "pretext with the subject nearby."

[8]Un., 7.22. The pun turns on the word *punnāga* which means both "white lotus" and "distinguished man," that is, Kṛṣṇa, who is standing right there. Kṛṣṇa then comes to her and says, "I heard your wish. Come, I will show you the white lotus." Taking her by the hand he leads to a bed made of white lotus blossoms. Her wish is fulfilled. (V)

यथा

तया निभृतमर्पिता मयि मुकुन्द सन्देशवाग्
व्रजाम्बुजदृशाद्य या श्रुतिपुटेन तां स्वीकुरु ।
प्रविश्य मम निर्भये यदिह सान्द्रनिद्रोत्सवे
कदर्थयसि धूर्त मां किमिव युक्तमेतत्तव ॥६०॥

yathā

tayā nibhṛtamarpitā mayi mukunda sandeśavāg
vrajāmbujadṛśādya yā śrutipuṭena tāṃ svīkuru |
praviśya mama nirbhaye yadiha sāndranidrotsave
kadarthayasi dhūrta māṃ kimiva yuktametattava ||60||

The letter carrier:

She entrusted me in private,
Mukunda, with the words of a message,
that lotus-eyed lady of Vraj.
Now accept them with the holes of your ears,
"You enter into the joys of my sleep,
when it is its most sound and deep,
and torment me, you crafty rogue.
Is this a worthy skill for you?"[9] (6)

---

[9]Un., 7.60. Rūpa defines the trusted messenger (*āptadūtī*) and gives her three types in the following way (7.54):

na viśrambhasya bhaṅgaṃ yā kuryāt prāṇātyayeṣv api |
snigdhā ca vāgminī cāsau dūtī syād gopasubhruvām |
amitārthā nisṛṣṭārthā patrahārīti sā tridhā ||

One who would not break confidence
Even to save her own life,
Affectionate and eloquent,
She is the messenger among
The ladies of the cowherders.
She is of three varieties:
Unlimited charges, bestowed charges,
And the carrier of letters.

After defining the message who has unlimited charges, and the messenger but one charge, Rūpa charaterizes the letter carrier (7.59):

sandeśamātraṃ yā yūnor nayet sā patrahārikā ||

She who brings only a message
For the two [Rādhā and Kṛṣṇa] is the letter carrier.

तत्र कृष्णप्रियायां वाच्यं, यथा

शप प्रहर तर्ज मां क्षिप बहिष्कुरुष्वाद्य वा
कदापि मतिराग्रहाय सखि मे विरंस्यत्यतः ।
प्रयामि तदहं हरेरुपनयाय सत्यं ब्रुवे
न सा श्वसितु या न वामनुभवेन्नवां सङ्गतिम् ॥७३॥

tatra kṛṣṇapriyāyāṃ vācyaṃ, yathā

śapa prahara tarja māṃ kṣipa bahiṣkuruṣvādya vā
kadāpi matirāgrahāya sakhi me viraṃsyatyataḥ |
prayāmi tadahaṃ harerupanayāya satyaṃ bruve
na sā śvasitu yā na vāmanubhavennavāṃ saṅgatim ||73||

A Message clearly stated to Kṛṣṇa's lover:

[*Tuṅgavidyā addresses this to Rādhā.* (V)]

Curse me, strike me, scold me, toss me,
or throw me out right now. My mind,
friend, being obstinate, will never give up.
Therefore, I am going to get Hari!
I tell you truthfully. She does not breathe
who does not want to see the two of you
in each other's embrace again.[10] (7)

---

[10]Un., 7.73. Rūpa identifies the various types of trusted messengers (7.61):

tāḥ śilpakārī daivajñā liṅginī paricārikā |
dhātreyī vanadevī ca sakhī cetyādayo vraje ||

They are an artist, fortune-teller,
female ascetic, servant, a daughter
of a nurse, a forest goddess,
a friend, and so forth in Vraja.

The female ascetic is referred to as *liṅginī*, "having a mark or sign, wearing a distinguishing mark," in this case, the mark or sign of renunciation.

Siṃhabhūpāla has a similar, though more extensive, list (1.160cd-161):

āsāṃ dūtyaḥ sakhī ceṭī liṅginī prativeśinī ||
dhātreyikā śilpakārī kumārī kathinī tathā |
kārur vipraśnikā ceti neṭṛmitraguṇānvitāḥ ||

The messengers of these [ladies]
are the friend, servant, ascetic,
neighbor, daughter of a nurse,
artist, young girl, story-teller,
artisan, and fortune-teller,
all on friendly terms with the hero.

Here, the messenger, Tuṅgavidyā, is a friend (*sakhī*) of Rādhā. Rūpa defines a friend as (7.70):

svātmano 'py adhikaṃ prema kurvāṇānyonyam acchalam |
viśrambhiṇī vayoveṣādibhis tulyā sakhī matā ||

They, without deceit, love one another
even more than they love themselves.
Trustworthy, alike in age, dress, and such,
they, indeed, are considered friends.

यथा वा

त्वमसि किमिव बाले व्याकुला तृष्णयोच्चैः
शृणु हितमविलम्बां तत्र यात्रां विधेहि ।
विलसदमलरागः पूर्वशैलस्य तिष्ठन्
विधुरुपरि चकोरि त्वत्प्रतीक्षां करोति ॥७५॥

yathā vā

tvamasi kimiva bāle vyākulā tṛṣṇayoccaiḥ
śṛṇu hitamavilambāṃ tatra yātrāṃ vidhehi |
vilasadamalarāgaḥ pūrvaśailasya tiṣṭhan
vidhurupari cakori tvatpratīkṣāṃ karoti ||75||

A suggested message:

[*Rādhā's confidant addresses this to a* cakorī, *a female partridge, on a branch of a nearby tree after determining where Kṛṣṇa waits for Rādhā.* (VG)]

Why are you, young thing, so perturbed
by your intense desire? Hear my advice.
Make your way there without delay.
For the moon is standing above
the eastern hill, glittering pure and red,
cakori, waiting just for you.[11] (8)

[11]Un., 7.75. The *cakora*, or Greek partridge, is fabled to subsist on moonbeams. Though addressed to the bird, the message is meant for Rādhā.

व्यपदेशेन

धवमुपेक्ष्य कठोरमियं पुरः
परिमलोल्लसिता किल माधवी ।
श्रयितुमुत्कलिकावलिताद्भुतं
ननु भवन्तमुपैति हलिप्रिय ॥८०॥

vyapadeśena

dhavamupekṣya kaṭhoramiyaṃ puraḥ
parimalollasitā kila mādhavī |
śrayitumutkalikāvalitādbhutaṃ
nanu bhavantamupaiti halipriya ||80||

Disguised suggestion in front of the beloved:

[*Viśākhā speaks to Kṛṣṇa.* (V)]

Rejecting the hard Dhava tree,
this spring jasmine in front of us,
bursting with fragrance, sporting fine blossoms,
marvelously, indeed, leans near—
to recline on you, Kadamba.[12] (9)

---

[12]Un., 7.80. Suggestion rests on double entendre here. The word *dhava* besides being a specific kind of tree also means "husband" and the word translated as *kadamba*, a kind of tree, is *halipriya*, "one dear to Baladeva," that is, Kṛṣṇa. Thus Rādhā is said to reject her hard husband in order to lean on Kṛṣṇa.

Rūpa earlier describes how messages are given to Kṛṣṇa by suggestion (*vyaṅgya*) (7.77):

tatpriyāyāḥ puraḥ paścāt
kṛṣṇe vyaṅgyaṃ dvidhā bhavet |
tatsākṣādvyapadeśābhyāṃ
dvividhaṃ ca dvidhoditam ||

Either in front of or behind
his beloved may one suggest
messages to Kṛṣṇa. And those
two are in turn two: suggestion
[made] directly or wrapped in disguise.

तत्प्रियायाः पश्चात्साक्षाद्व्यङ्ग्यं, यथा

स्फुरत्सुरमणिप्रभः सुरमणीघटाश्लाघितां
सदाभिमतसौरभः प्रकटसौरभोद्भासिनीम् ।
मुकुन्द मुदिरच्छविर्नवतडिच्छ्रियं तामसौ
भवानपि न चम्पकावलिमृते किल भ्राजते ॥८१॥

tatpriyāyāḥ paścātsākṣādvyaṅgyaṃ, yathā

sphuratsuramaṇiprabhaḥ suramaṇīghaṭāślāghitāṃ
sadābhimatasaurabhaḥ prakaṭasaurabhodbhāsinīm |
mukunda mudiracchavirnavataḍicchriyaṃ tāmasau
bhavānapi na campakāvalimṛte kila bhrājate ||81||

Direct suggestion behind his beloved's back:

[*A friend of Campakāvalī says this to Kṛṣṇa.* (V)]

You glow with that divine gem sparkling,
[but] she is lauded by ladies like jewels.
You are admired by [Indra's] fragrant cows,
[but] she is perfumed by fragrance itself.
Mukunda, you are the color of clouds,
[but] she has the loveliness of new lightning.
Even you, without Campakāvalī,
do not really manage to shine.[13] (10)

[13]Un., 7.81.

व्यपदेशेन व्यङ्ग्यं, यथा

शैलस्तुङ्गशिरा विराजति सरस्तस्योत्तरे विस्तृतं
तत्तीरे वनमुन्नतं तदुदरे हारी लतामण्डपः ।
तस्य द्वारि गभीरसौरभभरैराह्लादयन्ती दिशः
फुल्ला ते मधुसूदनाद्य पदवीमालोकते मालती ॥८२॥

vyapadeśena vyaṅgyaṃ, yathā

śailastuṅgaśirā virājati sarastasyottare vistṛtaṃ
tattīre vanamunnataṃ tadudare hārī latāmaṇḍapaḥ |
tasya dvāri gabhīrasaurabhabharairāhlādayantī diśaḥ
phullā te madhusūdanādya padavīmālokate mālatī ||82||

Dsiguised suggestion behind his beloved's back:

[*A dear friend of Rādhā addresses this to a honey bee in Kṛṣṇa's earshot.*]

A mountain shines with lofty peak;
and to its north spreads a broad lake.
On the lake's bank grows a tall wood.
In that wood hides a charmed arbor of vines.
At its door, pleasing all the directions
with the richness of her fragrance,
a jasmine bush in full blossom
watches the path on which you roam,
O collector of wild honey.[14] (11)

[14]Un., 7.82. The mountain is Govardhana; the lake is Rādhākuṇḍa. The collector of wild honey or honey bee (*madhusūdana*) is Kṛṣṇa, and the jasmine bush is Rādhikā. (V)

तत्र वाच्यं, यथा

त्वमसि मदसवो बहिश्चरन्तस्
त्वयि महती पटुता च वाग्मिता च ।
लघुरपि लघिमा न मे यथा स्यान्
मयि सखि रञ्जय माधवं तथाद्य ॥८७॥

tatra vācyaṃ, yathā

tvamasi madasavo bahiścarantas
tvayi mahatī paṭutā ca vāgmitā ca |
laghurapi laghimā na me yathā syān
mayi sakhi rañjaya mādhavaṃ tathādya ||87||

The directly expressed embassy of a friend:

[*Rādhā speaks to Viśākhā.* (V)]

You are my life breath moving outside me.
In you, too, are great skill and eloquence.
So that I do not become less than the least,
please, friend, make Mādhava love me.[15] (12)

---

[15]Un., 7.87.

तत्र शब्दमूलं, यथा

न हि शिक्षितुं वरकलासु कौशलं
गुणचातुरीं च न मृगाक्षि कामये ।
तमहं समभ्यसितुमेव सुभ्रुवां
सखि केशबन्धनविशेषमर्थये ॥८९॥

tatra śabdamūlaṃ, yathā

na hi śikṣituṃ varakalāsu kauśalaṃ
guṇacāturīṃ ca na mṛgākṣi kāmaye |
tamahaṃ samabhyasitumeva subhruvāṃ
sakhi keśabandhanaviśeṣamarthaye ||89||

Word-based suggestion:

[*Some cowherd lady says this to her companion.* (VG)]

I don't want to learn skill in the fine arts
nor, doe-eyed girl, dexterity with thread.
I want to practice, my friend, the special
way fine-browed ladies have of tying hair.[16] (13)

---

[16]Un., 7.89. "Special way of tying hair" is *keśa-bandhana-viśeṣam.* If one divides the word differently as in *keśavaṃ dhana-viśeṣam* one gets "Keśava [Kṛṣṇa], the special treasure." So while apparently telling her friend "I want to learn to tie hair," she is really telling her by suggestion "I want to cultivate Kṛṣṇa, who is a special treasure for me." One gets this by merely dividing the compound differently. Therefore, it is word-based suggestion as opposed to a meaning-based suggestion.

यथा वा

ण पौमराअप्पमुहं राणं कामेइ गोइ मे हिआम् ।
किन्तु सदा हीरबरं वाञ्छै हारन्तरे कादुम् ॥९०॥

[न पद्मरागप्रमुखं रत्नं कामयते गोपि मे हृदयम् ।
किन्तु सदा हीरवरं वाञ्छति हारान्तरे कर्तुम् ॥]

yathā vā

ṇa paumarāappamuhaṃ rāṇaṃ kāmei goi me hiām |
kintu sadā hīrabaraṃ vāñchai hārantare kādum ||90||

[na padmarāgapramukhaṃ ratnaṃ kāmayate gopi me hṛdayam |
kintu sadā hīravaraṃ vāñchati hārāntare kartum ||]

Another word-based suggestion:

[*Some bold village lady says this to a young, naive friend.* (VG)]

Cowherding girl, my heart does not want
a jewel, first and foremost a ruby.
But it always longs for the best diamond
to place inside my necklace.[17] (14)

---

[17]Un., 7.90. *Hīravara* means "the finest diamond." However, when preceded immediately by *sadā* ("always") it could also be *ahīravara*, "the best of cowherders," because of external euphonics or *sandhi*. The best of cowherders is Kṛṣṇa. This is a stanza in Prakrit with a Sanskrit "shadow" (*chāyā*) or version accompanying it.

तत्र स्वपत्याद्याक्षेपेण, यथा

विधातुर्दौरात्म्यान्न हि वहति घोरप्रकृतये
रुचिं चेतः पत्ये हतवपुरिदं दीव्यति रुचा ।
भजत्कक्षामक्ष्णोर्विषममिदमुग्रं प्रहरते
यमीतीरारण्यं किमिह सखि शिक्षां न तनुषे ॥९२॥

tatra svapatyādyākṣepeṇa, yathā

vidhāturdaurātmyānna hi vahati ghoraprakṛtaye
rucim cetaḥ patye hatavapuridaṃ dīvyati rucā |
bhajatkakṣāmakṣṇorviṣamamidamugraṃ praharate
yamītīrāraṇyaṃ kimiha sakhi śikṣāṃ na tanuṣe ||92||

Suggestion based on meaning tied to reviling one's husband:

[*Rādhā in prior passion* (pūrva-rāga) *addresses Viśākhā.* (V)]

Because of the creator's wickedness
my mind holds no liking for my husband
whose very nature is dreadful.
Yet this poor body shines with loveliness.
When I see them, these forests
on the bank of the sister of Yama,
vexatious and formidable,
[the sight] kills me. Friend,
have you no advice here?[18] (15)

---

[18]Un., 7.92. The suggested sense of this dialog stanza according to V is:

"What offense have I committed such that a husband with a deadful nature has been given to me? It is simply the creator's wickedness. It is not my fault if I have no liking for him. Truthfully, however, even if a husband with a beautiful nature had been given to me, I would not like him. My heart has been captured by Kṛṣṇa."

"But then let there be no attraction to your husband. Nevertheless, a chaste, family woman should not be attracted to another man."

"My body shines with youth and beauty and day by day it becomes more playful. It is the fault of this youthful body, not of my heart."

"You have a reputation and a sense of shame. You should disregard your nature and practice self-control."

"Before my eyes are these forests on the bank of this sister of Yama [the god of death] which assail me by igniting the flames of love, but never burning me up. Moreover, there are no means of calming me down. Nor are there any jewels, mantras, or medicines that have any influence here. In this, my time of distress, you have no advice for me?"

"There is no room for advice here."

"Then, after bidding farewell to family laws, shame, and reputation with offerings of water, quickly bring Kṛṣṇa here if you want to save my life."

गोविन्दादेः प्रशंसया, यथा

कुलस्त्रीणां नेष्टा परपुरुषरूपस्तुतिकथा
तथापि त्वं प्राणाः सखि मम वहिष्ठाः स्वयमसि ।
कियानास्ते तस्मिन्व्रजपतिकुमारे मधुरिमा
च्छटाप्याराद्यस्य म्रदयति दृशोर्द्वन्द्वममृतैः ॥९३॥

govindādeḥ praśaṃsayā, yathā

kulastrīṇāṃ neṣṭā parapuruṣarūpastutikathā
tathāpi tvaṃ prāṇāḥ sakhi mama vahiṣṭhāḥ svayamasi |
kiyānāste tasminvrajapatikumāre madhurimā
cchaṭāpyārādyasya mradayati dṛśordvandvamamṛtaiḥ ||93||

Suggestion based on meaning by praising Govinda:

[*Rādhā addresses Viśākhā here.* (V)]

Praising the beauty of a man
who is other than one's husband
is not approved in married women.
Still, friend, you are my very own life-force
situated outside of me.
How much sweetness there is in him,
the son of the Lord of Vraja!
Even a glimmer of it from afar
soothes my eyes with nectar.[19] (16)

---

[19]Un., 7.93

देशादि वैशिष्ट्येन, यथा

वृन्दारण्ये व्रततिपटलीसङ्कटे पुष्पहेतो-
र्भ्रामं भ्रामं सहचरि चिरं श्रान्तिमभ्यागतास्मि ।
तद्विश्रान्तिं क्षणमिह करोम्येकिकाहं निकुञ्जे
त्वं कालिन्दीतटपरिसरादाहरेथाः प्रसूनम् ॥९५॥

deśādi vaiśiṣṭyena, yathā

vṛndāraṇye vratatipaṭalīsaṅkaṭe puṣpaheto-
rbhrāmaṃ bhrāmaṃ sahacari ciraṃ śrāntimabhyāgatāsmi |
tadviśrāntiṃ kṣaṇamiha karomyekikāhaṃ nikuñje
tvaṃ kālindītaṭaparisarādāharethāḥ prasūnam ||95||

Suggestion based on meaning by the specialness of a place:

[*Some lady of Vraja says this to her accompanying friend.* (VG)]

Wandering for so long in Vṛndā's wood,
dense with masses of spreading vines,
gathering flowers,
I have become exhausted, friend.
Therefore, I will rest awhile here,
alone in this bower. Bring me
a blossom from the bank
of the Kālindī.[20] (17)

---

[20]Un., 7.95.

यथा वा

मधुरिता मधुना विधुनाप्यसौ
सखि पतङ्गसुतापुलिनाटवी ।
सवयसा वयसा च विभूषिता
तनुरियं किमिह क्षममुच्यताम् ॥९६॥

इति श्रीश्रीउज्ज्वलनीलमणौ दूतीभेदप्रकरणम् ॥७॥

yathā vā

madhuritā madhunā vidhunāpyasau
sakhi pataṅgasutāpulināṭavī |
savayasā vayasā ca vibhūṣitā
tanuriyaṃ kimiha kṣamamucyatām ||96||

iti śrīśrīujjvalanīlamaṇau dūtībhedaprakaraṇam ||7||

Suggestion based on meaning by the specialness of a place:

[*Rādhā addresses Viśākhā to test her cleverness.* (V)]

Sweetened by spring and now the moon,
Friend, is this shore-grove of the Sun's Daughter.[21]
Decorated also is this body
By youthful beauty and by a friend.
So tell me: what else is fitting here?[22] (18)

Thus ends Chapter Seven on the Messengers.

---

[21]The "Sun's Daughter" (*pataṅga-sutā*) is the River Yamunā.
[22]Un., 7.96.

Rādhā and Kṛṣṇa in Each Other's Clothes

The Devanāgarī Script and Pronunciation

Vowels: Sarveśvarāḥ/Svara

The sounds of the Sanksrit alphabet are divided among the different places in the mouth; a and ā are pronounced in the throat, i and ī at the palate, u and ū with the lips, ṛ and ṝ with the tongue curled upward at the roof of the mouth, ḷ and ḹ at the teeth, e at the palate, ai sliding from throat to palate, o at the lips, au sliding from throat to lips, and aḥ at the throat. (ă is a nasal sound)

अ — a, pronounced like "a" in "Roman,"[23]

आ — ā, pronounced like "a" in "father,"

इ — i, pronounced like "i" in "it" or "pin,"

ई — ī, pronounced like "i" in "police,"

उ — u, pronounced like "u" in "push,"

ऊ — ū, pronounced like "u" in "rude,"

[23]Many of these pronunciation examples s have been taken from the fine introduction to Sanskrit called *Sanskrit: an easy introduction to an enchanting language* by Ashok Aklujkar. (Richmond, British Columbia: Svādhyāya Publications, 1992)

ऋ — ṛ, pronounced like "er" in "fiber,"

ॠ — ṝ, pronounced like "ree" in "reel,"

ऌ — ḷ, pronounced like "le" in "angle,"

ॡ — ḹ, pronounced like "lea" in "leash,"

ए — e, pronounced like "ay" in "way,"

ऐ — ai, pronounced like "ai" in "aisle,"

ओ — o, pronounced like "o" in "note,"

औ — au, pronounced like "ow" in "now,"

आं — āṃ, pronounced like "ung" in "rung,"

आः — āḥ, pronounced like "aha,"

Consonants: Viṣṇujanāḥ/Vyañjana

The ka-varga (ka-group)

These velar consonants are all pronounced in the throat.

क् — k, pronounced like the "k" in "sky,"

ख् — kh, pronounced like "c" in "cat,"

ग् — g, pronounced like the "g" in "gum,"

घ् — gh, pronounced like the "gh" in "doghouse,"

ङ् — ṅ, pronounced like "ng" in "sung,"

The ca-varga (ca-group)

These palatal consonants are all pronounced at the palate.

च् — c, pronounced like the "ch" in "church,"

छ् — ch, pronounced like the "ch" in "chew,"

ज् — j, pronounced like "j" in "jump,"

झ् — jh, pronounce this like "j" with a strong outward breath,"

ञ् — ñ, pronounced like "n" in "canyon,"

The ṭa-varga (ṭa-group)

These retroflex consonants are all pronounced with the tip of the tongue curled upward touching the roof of the mouth.

ट् — ṭ, pronounced like the "t" in "art" or "stop,"

ठ् — ṭh, pronounced like the "th" in "boathouse,"

ड् — ḍ, pronounced like "d" in "ardent" or "bird,"

ढ् — ḍh, pronounce this like "dh" in "hardhat,"

ण् — ṇ, pronounced like "n" in "yarn," "land" or "tint,"

The ta-varga (ta-group)

These dental consonants are all pronounced at the teeth.

त् — t, pronounced like the "th" in "the," "them" or the french word "*tete* (head),

थ् — th, pronounced like the above letter 't', but with more aspiration,

द् — d, pronounced like in the french word "*donner*" (to give),

ध्— dh, pronounce this like "d" with a strong outward breath,

न्— n, pronounced like "n" in "no,"

The pa-varga (pa-group)

These labial consonants are all pronouced with the lips.

प्— p, pronounced like the "p" in "spin,"

फ् — pha, pronounced like the "ph" in "tophat,"

ब्— b, pronounced like "b" in "boat,"

भ्— bh, pronouned like "bh" in "abhor,"

म्— m, pronounced like "m" in "mud,"

The Semivowels: Harimitrāṇi

The sounds are divided thus; y is produced at the palate, r at the roof of the mouth, l at the teeth, and v at the lips.

य्— y, pronounced like the "y" in "yoga,"

र्— r, pronounced like the "r" in "relic,"

ल् — l, pronounced like "l" in "land,"

व्— v, pronounced like "v" in "vote,"

The Sibilants: Harigotrāṇi

The sounds are divided thus; ś is produced at the palate, ṣ at the roof of the mouth, s at the teeth, and h at the throat.

श्— ś, pronounced like the "sh" in "Swedish-chocolate,"

ष्— ṣ, pronounced with tongue curled upward touching the roof of the mouth,

स्— s, pronounced like "s" in "sun,"

ह् — h, pronounced like "h" in "house,"

Combining Vowels and Consonants

Most vowel consonant combinations follow the pattern shown here.

क्	+	अ	=	क
क्	+	आ	=	का
क्	+	इ	=	कि
क्	+	ई	=	की
क्	+	उ	=	कु
क्	+	ऊ	=	कू
क्	+	ऋ	=	कृ
क्	+	ॠ	=	कॄ
क्	+	ऌ	=	कॢ
क्	+	ॡ	=	कॣ
क्	+	ए	=	के
क्	+	ऐ	=	कै
क्	+	ओ	=	को
क्	+	औ	=	कौ

ग्	+	अ	=	ग
ग्	+	आ	=	गा
ग्	+	इ	=	गि
ग्	+	ई	=	गी
ग्	+	उ	=	गु
ग्	+	ऊ	=	गू
ग्	+	ऋ	=	गृ
ग्	+	ॠ	=	गॄ
ग्	+	ऌ	=	गॢ
ग्	+	ॡ	=	गॣ
ग्	+	ए	=	गे
ग्	+	ऐ	=	गै
ग्	+	ओ	=	गो
ग्	+	औ	=	गौ

And so forth.

Compound Consonants

क्क kka	क्ख kkha	क्च kca	क्ण kṇa	क्त kta
क्त्य ktya	क्त्र ktra	क्त्र्य ktrya	क्त्व ktva	क्न kna
क्न्य knya	क्म kma	क्य kya	क्र kra	क्र्य krya
क्ल kla	क्व kva	क्व्य kvya	क्ष kṣa	क्ष्म kṣma
क्ष्य kṣya	क्ष्व kṣva	ख्य khya	ख्र khra	ग्य gya
ग्र gra	ग्र्य grya	घ्न ghna	घ्न्य ghnya	घ्म ghma
घ्य ghya	घ्र ghra	ङ्क ṅka	ङ्त ṅta	ङ्क्त्य ṅktya
ङ्क्य ṅkya	ङ्क्ष ṅkṣa	ङ्क्ष्व ṅkṣva	ङ्ख ṅkha	ङ्ख्य ṅkhya
ङ्ग ṅga	ङ्ग्य ṅgya	ङ्घ ṅgha	ङ्घ्य ṅghya	ङ्घ्र ṅghra
ङ्ङ ṅṅa	ङ्न ṅna	ङ्म ṅma	ङ्य ṅya	च्च cca
च्छ ccha	च्छ्र cchra	च्ञ cña	च्म cma	च्य cya
छ्य chya	छ्र chra	ज्ज jja	ज्झ jjha	ज्ञ jña
ज्ञ्य jñya	ज्म jma	ज्य jya	ज्र jra	ज्व jva
ञ्च ñca	ञ्च्म ñcma	ञ्च्य ñcya	ञ्छ ñcha	ञ्ज ñja
ञ्ज्य ñjya	ट्ट ṭṭa	ट्य ṭya	ठ्य ṭhya	ठ्र ṭhra
ड्ग ḍga	ड्ग्य ḍgya	ड्घ ḍgha	ड्घ्र ḍghra	ड्ढ ḍḍha
ड्म ḍma	ड्य ḍya	ढ्य ḍhya	ढ्र ḍhra	ण्ट ṇṭa
ण्ठ ṇṭha	ण्ड ṇḍa	ण्ड्य ṇḍya	ण्ड्र ṇḍra	ण्ड्र्य ṇḍrya
ण्ढ ṇḍha	ण्ण ṇṇa	ण्म ṇma	ण्य ṇya	ण्व ṇva
त्क tka	त्क्र tkra	त्त tta	त्त्य ttya	त्त्र ttra
त्त्व ttva	त्थ ttha	त्न tna	त्न्य tnya	त्प tpa
त्प्र tpra	त्म tma	त्म्य tmya	त्य tya	त्र tra
त्र्य trya	त्व tva	त्स tsa	त्स्न tsna	त्स्न्य tsnya
थ्य thya	द्ग dga	द्ग्र dgra	द्घ dgha	द्घ्र dghra
द्द dda	द्द्य ddya	द्ध ddha	द्ध्य ddhya	द्न dna
द्ब dba	द्भ dbha	द्भ्य dbhya	द्म dma	द्य dya
द्र dra	द्र्य drya	द्व dva	द्व्य dvya	ध्न dhna
ध्न्य dhnya	ध्म dhma	ध्य dhya	ध्र dhra	ध्र्य dhrya
ध्व dhva	न्त nta	न्त्य ntya	न्त्र ntra	न्द nda
न्द्र ndra	न्ध ndha	न्ध्र ndhra	न्न nna	न्प npa
न्प्र npra	न्म nma	न्य nya	न्र nra	न्स nsa
प्त pta	प्त्य ptya	प्न pna	प्प ppa	प्म pma
प्य pya	प्र pra	प्ल pla	प्व pva	प्स psa
प्स्व psva	ब्घ bgha	ब्ज bja	ब्द bda	ब्ध bdha

ब्न bna	ब्ब bba	ब्भ bbha	ब्भ्य bbhya	ब्य bya
ब्र bra	ब्व bva	भ्न bhna	भ्य bhya	भ्र bhra
भ्व bhva	म्र mra	म्प mpa	म्प्र mpra	म्ब mba
म्भ mbha	म्म mma	म्य mya	म्न mna	म्ल mla
म्व mva	य्य yya	य्व yva	ल्क lka	ल्प lpa
ल्म lma	ल्य lya	ल्ल lla	ल्व lva	ल्ह lha
व्न vna	व्य vya	व्र vra	व्व vva	श्च śca
श्च्य ścya	श्न śna	श्य śya	श्र śra	श्र्य śrya
श्ल śla	श्व śva	श्व्य śvya	श्श śśa	ष्ट ṣṭa
ष्ट्य ṣṭya	ष्ट्र ṣṭra	ष्ट्र्य ṣṭrya	ष्ट्व ṣṭva	ष्ठ ṣṭha
ष्ण ṣṇa	ष्ण्य ṣṇya	ष्प ṣpa	ष्प्र ṣpra	ष्म ṣma
ष्य ṣya	ष्व ṣva	स्क ska	स्ख skha	स्त sta
स्त्य stya	स्त्र stra	स्त्व stv	स्थ stha	स्न sna
स्न्य snya	स्प spa	स्फ spha	स्म sma	स्म्य smya
स्य sya	स्र sra	स्व sva	स्स ssa	ह्ण hṇa
ह्न hna	ह्म hma	ह्य hya	ह्र hra	ह्ल hla
ह्व hva				

Pronunciation Table

	guttural	palatal	retroflex	dental	labial
Short vowels	अ (a)	इ (i)	ऋ (ṛ)	ऌ (ḷ)	उ (u)
Long vowels	आ (ā)	ई (ī), ए (e)	ॠ (ṝ)	ॡ (ḹ)	ऊ (ū), ओ (o)
Unvoiced, unaspirated	क (ka)	च (ca)	ट (ṭa)	त (ta)	प (pa)
Unvoiced, aspirated	ख (kha)	छ (cha)	ठ (ṭha)	थ (tha)	फ (pha)
Voiced, unaspirated	ग (g)	ज (ja)	ड (ḍa)	द (da)	ब (ba)
Voiced, aspirated	घ (gha)	झ (jha)	ढ (ḍha)	ध (dha)	भ (bha)
Nasals	ङ (ṅa)	ञ (ña)	ण (ṇa)	न (na)	म (ma)
Semivowels		य (ya)	र (ra)	ल (la)	व (va)
Sibilants	ह (ha)	श (śa)	ष (ṣa)	स (sa)	

ऐ (ai) slides from guttural to palatal.
औ (au) slides from guttural to labial.

Bibliography

Ānandavardhana. *Dhvanyāloka.* Delhi, India: Motilal Banarsidass, 1982, 2nd edition. In Sanskrit with English translation by Dr. K. Krishnamoorthy. Foreword by Dr. K. R. Srinivasa Iyengar.

———. *Dhvanyāloka o Locana.* Kalakātā, India: Mukhārjī āṇḍa Koṃ Prāḥ Liḥ, 1986, 2nd edition. In Sanskrit with Bengali translation by Subodhacandra Sengupta. Edited by Kālīpada Bhaṭṭācārya.

Bharatamuni. *Nāṭya Śāstra of Bharatamuni,* volume 1. Delhi, India: Parimal Publications, 1981, 1st edition. In Sanskrit with English introduction. Includes the commentary of Abhinavagupta called *Abhinavabhāratī.* Vol. 1 contains Chapters 1-7.

———. *The Natya Sastra of Bharatamuni.* Delhi, India: Sri Satguru Publications, 1987 [Repr.]. English translation by Board of Scholars.

Brzezinski, Jan. "Does Kṛṣṇa Marry the Gopīs in the End?" *Journal of Vaiṣṇava Studies* 5.4. Pages 49-110.

De, Sushil Kumar. *Early History the Vaiṣṇava Faith and Movement in Bengal.* Calcutta, India: Firma KLM Private Limited, 1986 [Repr.].

Delmonico, Neal, editor. *Gifts of Sacred Wonder.* Calcutta, India: Subarnarekha, 1986, 1st edition. Essays by various authors on aspects of the Caitanya Vaiṣṇava tradition.

Delmonico, Neal. "Sacred Rapture: the *Bhakti-rasa* Theory of Rūpa Gosvāmin." *Shaping Bengali Worlds, Public and Private* 15.1 (1989). Pages 1-7. Volume edited by Tony K. Stewart.

———. *Sacred Rapture: A Study of the Religious Aesthetic of Śrī Rūpa Gosvāmin.* Ph.D. thesis, University of Chicago, Chicago, IL, 1990.

———. "Rūpa Gosvāmin: His Life, Family, and Early Vraja Commentators." *Journal of Vaiṣṇava Studies* 1.2 (1993). Pages 133-157.

———. *How to Partake in the Love of Kṛṣṇa.*, Princeton, NJ: Printon University Press, 1995, 244–68. 1st edition.

———. "The Blazing Sapphire (*Ujjvala-nīla-maṇi*)." *Journal of Vaiṣṇava Studies* 5.1 (1996-7). Pages 21-52.

———. "Rādhā: the Quintessential Gopī (The Fourth Chapter of Rūpa Gosvāmin's *Ujjvala-nīlamaṇi*)." *Journal of Vaiṣṇava Studies* 5.4 (1997). Pages 111-137.

———. "Sacred Rapture: the *Bhakti-rasa* Theory of Rūpa Gosvāmin." *Journal of Vaiṣṇava Studies* 6.1 (1998). Pages 75-98.

———. "Trouble in Paradise: a Confict in the Caitanya Vaiṣṇava Tradition." *Journal of Vaiṣṇava Studies* 8.1 (1999). Pages 91-101.

———. "Rādhā's Bath: an excerpt from *Govinda-līlāmṛta.*" *Journal of Vaiṣṇava Studies* 10.1 (2001). Pages 81-90.

———. "Re-assembling the Giant: the Development of Monotheism in Vaiṣṇava Theology." *Journal of Vaiṣṇava Studies* 13.1 (2004). Pages 155-177.

———. "The Vedic Puruṣa and Vaiṣṇavism." *Journal of Vaiṣṇava Studies* 15.1 (2006). Pages 125-151.

Delmonico, Neal, editor. *The Divine Song, or Bhagavad-gītā.* Kirksville, MO: Blazing Sapphire Press, 2012, 1st edition. In Sanskrit with English translation by C.C. Caleb. Notes based on Śaṅkara's commentary. Six traditional summaries of the Gītā in an appendix.

Dhanañjaya. *Daśarūpakaḥ.* New York: Columbia University, 1912, 1st edition. In English with Sanskrit in transliteration. Translated by George C. O. Haas.

Gnoli, Raniero. *The Aesthetic Experience according to Abhinava Gupta.* Varanasi: Chowkhamba Sanskrit Series Office, 1968, 1st edition. English translation with original Sanskrit in transliteration.

Gosvāmin, Jīva. *Śrī-bhakti-śrīprīti-nāmaka-sandarbhadvayam.* Vṛndāvana, India: Haridāsa Śarmā, 1951a, 1st edition. In Sanskrit (Bengali script). Edited by Purīdāsa Mahāśaya.

———. *Śrī-tattva-śrībhagavat-śrīparamātma-śrīkṛṣṇākhya-sandarbha-catuṣṭayam.* Vṛndāvana, India: Haridāsa Śarmā, 1951b, 1st edition. In Sanskrit (Bengali script). Edited by Purīdāsa Mahāśaya.

———. *Śrī Śrī Sarvasaṃvādinī.* Vṛndāvana, India: Haridāsa Śarman, 1953, 1st edition. In Sanskrit (Bengali script). A commentary on the author's first four *sandarbhas*: *Tattva, Bhagavat, Paramātma,* and *Kṛṣṇa.*

———. *Śrī Bhagavatsandarbha.* Vṛndāvana, India: Sadgranthaprakāśaka, 1983, 1st edition. In Sanskrit (Devanāgarī script) with a Hindi trans. The second of the six *sandarbhas* or treatises by Jīva that make up the Caitanya tradition's major set of theological dogmas. Edited with Jīva's autocommentary *Sarvasaṃvādinī* by Haridāsa Śāstrī.

Gosvāmin, Raghunātha Dāsa. *Stavāvalī.* Mūrśidābād (West Bengal, India): Rādhāramaṇa Yantra, 1923 [1329], 2nd edition. In Sanskrit with the commentary of Vaṅgeśvara Vidyābhūṣaṇa and a Bengali translation.

Gosvāmin, Rūpa. *Ujjvala-nīla-maṇiḥ.* Varahampura, West Bengal, India: Vrajanātha Miśra, 1925, 3rd edition. In Sanskrit (Bengali script) with a Bengali translation. With the commentaries of Jīva Gosvāmin and Viśvanātha Cakravartin. Edited and translated by Rāmanārāyaṇa Vidyāratna.

———. *Ujjvala-nīla-maṇiḥ.* Vṛndāvanadhāma, India: Haridāsa Śarma, 1954a, 1st edition. In Sanskrit (Bengali script). With the commentaries of Jīva Gosvāmin and Viśvanātha Cakravartin. Edited by Purīdāsa.

———. *Ujjvala-nīla-maṇiḥ.* Kusumasarovara, Vraja, India: Kṛṣṇadāsa Bābā, 1954b, 1st edition. In Sanskrit with Hindi translation based on the commentaries of Jīva Gosvāmin and Viśvanātha Cakravartin. Translated by Kṛṣṇadāsa Bābā.

———. *Śrīpadyāvalī*. Vṛndāvana, India: Rāghavacaitanyadāsa, 1959, 1st edition. In Sanskrit with Hindi translation by Vanamālidāsa Śāstrī.

———. *Nāṭaka-candrikā*. Varanasi, India: Chowkhamba Sanskrit Series Office, 1964, 1st edition. In Sanskrit with Hindi translation by Bābūlāla Śukla Śāstrī.

———. *Ujjvala-nīla-maṇiḥ*. Navadvīpa, West Bengal, India: Mukundadāsa, 1964 [G. 478], 2nd edition. In Sanskrit (Bengali script) with a Bengali translation. Edited with the commentary of Viṣṇudāsa Gosvāmin by Haridāsa Dāsa.

———. *Śrī Śrī Bhakti-rasāmṛtra-sindhuḥ*. Mathurā, India: Śrī Kṛṣṇajanmasthāna, 1981 [G. 495], 3rd edition. Edited with the commentaries of Śrī Jīva, Mukundadāsa, and Viśvanātha Cakravartin and a Bengali translation by Haridāsa Dāsa. In Sanskrit and Bengali.

———. *Ujjvala-nīla-maṇi*. Varanasi, India: Chaukhamba Sanskrit Pratishthan, 1985 [Repr.]. In Sanskrit (Devanāgarī script). Edited with the commentaries of Jīvagosvāmin and Viśvanātha Chakravarty by M. M. Pandit Durga Prasad & Vasudev Lakshaman Shastri Panashikar.

———. *The Bhakti-rasāmṛta-sindhu of Rūpa Gosvāmin*. New Delhi, India: Indira Gandhi Center for the Arts, 2003, 1st edition. Translated into English with introduction and notes by David L. Haberman.

Gosvāmin, Sanātana. *Bṛhad-bhāgavatāmṛta*. Mayamanasiṃha (now in Bangladesh): Śacīnātharāya, 1944 [G. 458], 1st edition. In Sanskrit (Bengali script). Edited with the author's own commentary by Purīdāsa.

Gosvāmī, Kānupriya. *On Associating with Great Ones*. Kirksville, Missouri, USA: Blazing Sapphire Press, 2014, 1st edition. In English. Translation of *Mahat-saṅga Prasaṅga* (1970) by Kānupriya Gosvāmin, on the transmission of *bhakti* for Kṛṣṇa through association with men and women who are *bhaktas*. Translated by Neal Delmonico from the Bengali.

Haberman, David L. *Acting as a Way of Salvation: a Study of Rāgānuga Bhakti Sādhana*. New York, NY: Oxford University Press, 1988, 1st edition.

Heidegger, Martin. *Nietzsche: The Will to Power as Art.* San Francisco: Harper & Row, 1979, 1st edition. Translated from the German with notes and an analysis by David Farrell Krell.

Jānā, Nareścandra. *Vṛndāvaner Chaẏa Gosvāmī.* Calcutta, India: Kalikātā Viśvavidyālaya, 1970, 1st edition.

Kavirāja, Kṛṣṇadāsa. *The Caitanya Caritāmṛta of Kṛṣṇadāsa Kaviraja.* Kalikātā, India: Devakīnandana Dharmaprakāśa Kāryālaya, 1931 [1337], 3rd edition. In Bengali. With commentary, notes, and translation of the Sanskrit stanzas into Bengali by Prabhupāda Rādhikānātha Gosvāmī.

———. *Caitanya-caritāmṛta.* Kalikātā: Sādhanā Prakāśanī, 1963 [], 4th edition. In Bengali and Sanskrit. Complete in six volumes. Edited with commentary by Dr. Rādhāgovinda Nātha.

———. *The Caitanya Caritāmṛta of Kṛṣṇadāsa Kaviraja.* Cambridge, MA: Department of Sanskrit and Indian Studies, Harvard University, 1999, 1st edition. A translation and commentary by Edward C. Dimock, Jr. Edited by Tony K. Stewart.

Kavirāja, Viśvanātha. *Sāhiya-darpaṇa.* Kalikātā, India: Saṃskṛta Pusṭaka Bhāṇḍāra, 1992 [1386], 2nd edition. In Sanskrit (Bengali script). Edited and translated into Bengali by Vimalākānta Mukhopādhyāya with the commentary of Rāmacaraṇa Tarkavāgīśa.

Mahāprabhu, Śrī Caitanya. *Śrī Caitanya-śikṣāṣṭakam.* Vṛndāvana, India: Śrī Sāvitrī Guha, 1984, 2nd edition. In Sanskrit (Bengali script) with Bengali translation and commentary. Eight verses said to have been composed by Caitanya. Translated with the Bengali commentary of Śrī Maṇīndranātha Guha.

———. *Śrī Śrī Śikṣāṣṭakam.* Rādhākuṇḍa, India: Śrī Ananta Dāsa Bābājī Mahārāja, 2003, 1st edition. Eight verses said to have been composed by Caitanya. With the commentary of Ananta Dāsa Bābājī Mahārāja. Translated into English by Advaita Das.

Majumdār, Vimanavihārī. *Śrī Caitanyacariter Upādāna.* Calcutta, India: Kalikātā Viśvavidyālaya, 1959, 2nd edition.

Mukhopādhyāya, Sukhamaya. *Bāṃlāra Itihāsera Du'śo Bachara.* Kalikātā, India: Bhāratī Book Stall, 1962, 1st edition.

———. *Madhyayugera Bāṃlā Sāhityera Tathya o Kāla-krama*. Kalikātā, India: G. Bhāradvāja and Co., 1974, 1st edition.

Purīdāsa, editor. *Śrīmad-bhāgavatam*. Mayamanasiṃha, Bangla Desh: Śacīnātharāya-caturdhurīṇa, 1945, 1st edition. In Sanskrit. No commentaries. Complete in three volumes.

Rāyacaudhurī, Girijāśaṅkara. *Śrī Caitanya o Tā̃hār Pārṣadagaṇa*. Calcutta, India: Kalikātā Viśvavidyālaya, 1957, 1st edition. In Bengali.

Sarma, Sreeramula Rajeswara. "Tṛtīyakaḥ phenakaḥ." *Journal of European Ayurvedic Society* 2 (1992). Pages 115-123.

Śāstrī, Bhagavat Kumar. *The Bhakti Cult in Ancient India*. Varanasi, India: The Chowkhamba Sanskrit Series Office, 1965, 2nd edition.

Siṃhabhūpāla. *Rasārṇavasudhākara*. Madras, India: The Adyar Library and Research Centre, 1979, 1st edition. In Sanskrit (Devanagari script).

Stewart, Tony K. *The Final Word: The Caitanya-caritāmṛta and the Grammar of Religious Tradition*. New York, NY: Oxford University Press, 2010, 1st edition.

Vidyābhūṣaṇa, Baladeva. *Siddhāntaratna*. Benares, India: Government Sanskrit Library, 1927, 1st edition. In Sanskrit (Devanāgarī) with the autocommentary of Baladeva. Two volumes. Edited by Gopīnātha Kavirāja in the Princess of Wales Saraswati Bhavana Texts series (no. 10).

Warder, A. K. *Indian Kāvya Literature*, volume 1. Delhi, India: Motilal Banarsidass, 1989, 1st edition.

Zacks, Jeffrey. *Flicker: Your Brain on Movies*. Oxford: Oxford University Press, 2014, 1st edition.

Other Books by Blazing Sapphire Press

1. *Experiences in Bhakti: the Science Celestial* by Dr. O. B. L. Kapoor. This book is on the empirical dimensions of the Vaiṣṇava religious tradition centered around the worship of the Hindu god Kṛṣṇa. It uses stories from the lives of the saints of the tradition, large and small, to suggest that Vaiṣṇavism has many similarities with modern science and can be thought of as a kind of science. (ISBN: 978-0-9817902-6-8, soft; 978-0-9747968-6-4, hard)

2. *Fundamentals of Vedānta*, Part 1: *The Vedānta-sāra* of Sadānanda Yogīndra and the *Prameya-ratnāvalī* of Baladeva Vidyābhūṣaṇa (trans. by Neal Delmonico). *Fundamentals of Vedānta*, Part One, is a translation, with a detailed introduction and notes, of two short Sanskrit texts, the *Vedānta-sāra* (Essence of Vedānta) of Sadānanda and the *Prameya-ratnāvalī* (Necklace of Truth-Jewels) of Baladeva, from opposite ends of the Vedāntic spectrum. Each has been used in India for centuries to introduce beginning students to the fundamental ideas of Vedānta. (ISBN: 978-0-9747968-3-3)

3. *Īśopaniṣad*. A new literal and poetic translation of this seminal Vedānta text by Neal Delmonico and Lloyd Pflueger with introduction, the original text in Devanagari and transliteration, facing glossary with grammatical notes, contrasting traditional commentaries of Śaṅkara and Madhva, scholarly notes with recent research, a brief introduction to the Sanskrit language, index and bibliography, and study questions for classroom and thoughtful inquiry. (ISBN: 978-1-936135-09-7, soft; 978-1-936135-29-5,

hard)

4. *The Life and Teachings of Krishna Das Baba of Radhakund* by Zakrent Christian. This is a work on the life and teachings of a 20th century saint from the Caitanya Vaiṣṇava tradition. Krishna Das Baba was a well known practitioner and guide who lived in a community of renunciants nestled around a holy lake in North India called Radhakund (the Pond of Śrī Rādhā). His story is typical of many stories of modern Indian men and women who gave up participation in modern society to pursue religious and spiritual goals. It thus presents insight into the yearnings of many modern Indians who when faced with the challenges of modernity haved turned towards tradition. (ISBN: 978-0-9747968-5-7)

5. *Nectar of the Holy Name* by Manindranath Guha (trans. Neal Delmonico). This is a translation of Manindranath Guha's classic Bengali book, the *Hari-nāmāmṛta-sindhu-bindu*, on the beliefs and practices of the repeating the "holy names" (the names of Kṛṣṇa and of his consort Rādhā) of the Caitanya Vaiṣṇava tradition. Guha's book is a good introduction to an area of theological reflection in Caitanya Vaiṣṇavism called the "theology of the holy name." (ISBN: 978-0-9747968-1-9, soft; 978-0-9747968-2-6, hard)

6. *On Associating with Great Ones* by Kānupriya Gosvāmī (trans. Neal Delmonico). This is a translation of Kānupriya Gosvāmīs Bengali book, *Mahat-saṅga Prasaṅga.* This volume contains some of Kānupriya Gosvāmī's lectures on the topic of the uplifting power of associating, that is, meeting and conversing, with the holy men and women (*sādhus* and *sādhvīs*) of the Caitanya tradition. The essays were recorded, arranged, and edited by Kānupriya Gosvāmī's nephew, Gauraray Das Goswami. (ISBN:978-0-9817902-9-9, soft)

7. *Sādhu Sādhu: a Life of Baba Śrī Tinkudi Gosvami* by Binode Bihari Dasa Babaji. This is an English translation of Śrī Binode Bihari Das Babaji's short Bengali work on the life of Baba Tinkudi Goswami, one of the great Vaiṣṇava practitioners and saints of the 20th century. This work is translated by Neal Delmonico with an introduction and annotations. It also contains two Bengali songs by his disciples remembering Tinkudi Goswami's life

and some short recollections of him by some of his American disciples. (ISBN: 978-0-9747968-8-8)

8. *The Song Divine, or Bhagavad-gītā: a Metrical Rendering (with Annotations)* (English and Sanskrit edition), trans. by C.C. Caleb. This is a new edition of the delightful English metrical translation by C.C. Caleb of the Hindu classic, the *Bhagavad-gītā,* with an introduction, annotations, and an appendix. The original Sanskrit text, in both Devanāgarī and transliteration, of the *Gītā* has been included on the left hand pages for easy access and comparison with the translation. An appendix has been added containing short summaries of the teachings of the *Gītā* by many of the great commentators on the text: Śaṅkara, Yamunā Muni, Rāmānuja, Madhusūdana Sarasvatī, Viśvanātha Cakravartin, and Baladeva Vidyābhūṣaṇa. (ISBN: 978-0-9817902-3-7)

9. *The Song Divine, or Bhagavad-Gita: A Metrical Rendering (with Annotations) (English-only Edition)* trans. by C.C. Caleb. This is an edition of the metrical English translation by C.C. Caleb of the great Hindu classic, the *Bhagavad-gītā,* or The Song Divine. It includes an introduction to the text, annotations drawn from the commentary of Śaṅkara, and an appendix containing some of the traditional summaries of the text from different schools of interpretation. This edition does not include the original Sanskrit text of the *Gītā.* (ISBN: 978-0-9817902-8-2)

10. *Śrī Kṛṣṇa, the Lord of Love,* Premananda Bharati. Premananda Bharati's classic work, *Sri Krishna: the Lord of Love,* was originally published in 1904 in New York. It is the first full-length work presenting theistic Hindu practices and beliefs before a Western audience by a practicing Hindu "missionary." Premananda Bharati or Baba (Father) Bharati had come to the USA as a result of the encouragement of his co-religionists in India and of a vision he received while living in a pilgrimage site sacred to his tradition. He arrived in the USA in 1902 and stayed until 1911 with one return journey to India in 1907 with several of his American disciples. His book was read and admired by numerous American and British men and women of the early 20th century and captured the attention of the great Russian writer Leo Tolstoy through whom Mahatma Gandhi discovered it. This new edi-

tion contains two introductions, one by Gerald T. Carney, PhD, a specialist on Premananda Bharati's life and work and another by Neal Delmonico, PhD, a specialist on Caitanya Vaiṣṇavism, the religious tradition to which Baba Bharati belonged. In addition, the text has been edited, corrected, annotated, and newly typeset. Appendices have been added containing supporting texts and additional materials bearing on Baba Bharati's sources for some of the ideas in his book and on his life and practices in India before his arrival in the USA. (ISBN: 978-0-9747968-7-1)

11. *Śrīmad-Bhagavad-Gītā (Sanskrit Edition)* ed. and introduced by Neal Delmonico. This is an edition of the *Bhagavad-gītā* in the original language of the text, Sanskrit. No translation of the text is given in this book. Only a Roman transliteration is provided alongside the Devanāgarī version and a number of the most common variant readings in footnotes. There are hundreds of translations of the *Gītā* in various of the languages of the world and some of them include the text in either its native script, which is called Devanāgarī (the city of the gods), or in some transliterated format. A few even include word-by-word translations. But, many translations include neither text nor word equivalences. This edition is for those who would like to have access to and get to know the text itself better. It can be paired with any of the translations available in any language, including our own companion volume called the *The Song Divine*, which is a reprint/re-edition of the old classic verse translation of C. C. Caleb completed in India in 1911. (ISBN: 079-1-936135-00-4)

12. *Vaishnava Temple Music in Vrindaban: the Radhavallabha Songbook* by Guy L. Beck. This is a collection of 108 songs from the Radhavallabha tradition, a major North Indian *bhakti* tradition dating from the 16th century. The songs have been collected by ethno-musicologist Guy L Beck over a period of thirty years during which time he paid many visits to the religious headquarters of the sect, in Vrindaban, UP, India. In the book, Beck analyzes each song, discussing its rhythmic characteristics and its melodic structure within the raga system of classical Indian music. The verbal text for each song is given along with a faithful translation into English. In a long introduction, Beck discusses the development of religious music in India with reference to the special

history and contributions of the Radhavallabha tradition. Two CDs filled with recordings of sample music are available free to purchasers of the book and the entire collection of recordings covering 18 expertly mastered CDs is available for purchase separately. (ISBN: 978-0-9817902-4-4)

Coming soon:

1. *The Blazing Sapphire (Ujjvala-nīlamaṇi)* by Rūpa Gosvāmin (full translation by Neal and Betsy Delmonico). In multiple volumes. In Sanskrit and English with introduction, notes, and the commentaries of Jīva Gosvāmin, Viṣṇudāsa Gosvāmin, and Viśvanātha Cakravartin.

2. *My Gurudeva: a short biography of Siddha Manohara Dāsa Bābājī* by Navadvīpa Dāsa with excerpts from the original works of Siddha Manohara Dāsa Bābā. Translation, introduction, and annotation by Neal Delmonico.

3. *In Praise of Kṛṣṇa's Sports (Kṛṣṇa-līlā-stava)*, the first theological/-meditational text of the Caitanya Vaiṣṇava tradition, by Sanātana Gosvāmī. Translation, introduction, and annotation by Neal Delmonico.

4. *Sacred Rapture: a Study of the Religious Aesthetic of Śrī Rūpa Gosvāmin* by Neal Delmonico.

5. *The Eight Instructions of Caitanya (Caitanya-śikṣāṣṭaka)* with the Bengali commentary of Manindranath Guha. Translated, introduced, and annotated by Neal Delmonico.

6. *Holy Name—Thought Jewel (Nāma-cintāmaṇi)* by Kānupriya Gosvāmī. In three volumes. Translated, introduced, and annotated by Neal Delmonico

7. *Mahāmantra (The Great Mantra)* by Sundarānanda Dāsa Vidyāvinoda. Translated, introduced, and annotated by Neal Delmonico.

8. *Moonlight on the Daily Acts of Kṛṣṇa (Kṛṣṇāhnika-kaumudī)* , the earliest meditation/visualization (*līlā-smaraṇa*) text of the Cai-

tanya tradition, by Kavikarṇapūra. Translated, introduced, and annotated by Neal Delmonico.

Introducing Golden Avatar Press

1. *Gosvāmins of Vṛndāvana* by Dr. O.B.L. Kapoor. (coming soon)

2. *Lord Gaurāṅga, or Salvation for All* by Shishir Kumar Ghosh. 2 vols. (coming soon)

www.ingramcontent.com/pod-product-compliance
Lightning Source LLC
Chambersburg PA
CBHW071600080526
44588CB00010B/966
* 9 7 8 1 9 3 6 1 3 5 3 5 6 *